Y0-DVF-755

The Theatre Student
SCENES TO PERFORM

THE THEATRE STUDENT SERIES

The Theatre Student
SCENES TO PERFORM

Peter Kline

PUBLISHED BY
RICHARDS ROSEN PRESS, INC.
NEW YORK, N.Y. 10010

Wingate College Library

Standard Book Number 8239–0176–9 Sept. 13, 1975
Library of Congress Catalog Card Number: 69–11716
Dewey Decimal Classification: 792

Published in 1969 by Richards Rosen Press, Inc.
29 East 21st Street, New York City, N.Y. 10010

Copyright 1969 by Peter Kline

All rights reserved. No part of this book
may be reproduced in any form without written
permission from the publisher, except by a reviewer.

Revised Edition

Manufactured in the United States of America

ACKNOWLEDGMENTS

The author wishes to express his indebtedness to Joseph W. Donohue, Jr., and *Theatre Notebook* for permission to quote from Dr. Donohue's article, "Kemble and Mrs. Siddons in *Macbeth:* The Romantic Approach to Tragic Character," and to the Garrick Club, *Theatre Notebook,* and Dr. Donohue for permission to use the portrait of Mrs. Siddons as Lady Macbeth.

DEDICATION

For my wife,
whose much appreciated assistance is reflected in this book in many ways.

ABOUT THE AUTHOR

Peter Kline has taught acting and speech to high-school and college students for the past ten years. During that time he has been head of the English department, with full responsibility for dramatic activities, at the Maret School in Washington, D.C., and at Sandy Spring Friends School in Sandy Spring, Maryland. He also has taught speech and drama at Dunbarton College, acted as director for the Valerie Warde Drama School, and directed religious drama for two churches. He has directed more than fifty major productions, most of them plays in the category of classical drama. From 1951 to 1965 he combined the roles of actor, director, and producer with the Lyric Theater Company, which he founded to produce Gilbert and Sullivan operas during the summer months. Its recordings of such little-known works as *Utopia, Ltd., The Grand Duke,* and *The Mountebanks* have been sold throughout the world and received critical acclaim. He is the author of a number of plays, one of which, a dramatization of George Eliot's *Romola,* has been professionally recorded and broadcast.

Kline received his B.A. from Amherst College in 1957, and his M.A. from Catholic University in 1960, both in speech and drama. He is married and has three children.

Throughout his career, Kline has sought to combine the discipline of dramatic tradition with the freedom of individual self-expression. He believes that the actor should recreate in his imagination the attitudes and values of the playwright, but give expression to those attitudes and values through his own personality. Only when he has accepted the discipline of responsibility to the playwright's intentions can the actor be truly creative.

CONTENTS

Introduction	13
To the Student	15
To the Teacher	19
SCENES FOR MEN:	
Everyman's Prayer, from *Everyman*	25
The Death of Zenocrate, from *Tamburlaine the Great*	33
Richard Alone, from *Richard III*	43
To Be or Not to Be, from *Hamlet*	53
Harpagon Searches for His Stolen Money, from *The Miser*	63
Lord Foppington's Day, from *The Relapse*	71
My Last Duchess	81
Nose Speech, from *Cyrano de Bergerac*	93
Peer Gynt Leaves Solveig, from *Peer Gynt*	103
SCENES FOR WOMEN:	
Katherina's Obedience, from *The Taming of the Shrew*	111
Lady Macbeth Receives a Letter from Her Husband, from *Macbeth*	121
Cleopatra's Death Scene, from *Antony and Cleopatra*	133
The Jailer's Daughter Falls in Love with a Prince, from *The Two Noble Kinsmen*	141
Eve Decides to Eat the Fruit of the Tree of Knowledge, from *Paradise Lost*	151
Belinda Bemoans the Loss of a Lock of Her Hair, from *The Rape of the Lock*	163
Aase Searches for Her Son, from *Peer Gynt*	173
On Being Too Frequently Proposed to, from *An Ideal Husband*	181
Bibliography	189

EDITOR'S NOTE

There are several ways to learn a performing art. One way is to start with outer technique and proceed to the creation of correct inner emotional states. This is the method of ballet and music training. Another method is to create compelling inner motivation and then develop outer technique.

The method proposed by Peter Kline in this book starts with the outer technique in the expectation that a proper emotional and intellectual response will follow. This method brings quick results and is suitable for large classes. Best of all, this method provides a form or boundary for the student, which gives him security and specific objectives. At the same time, it encourages freedom of expression and individual interpretation. It will be an excellent introduction to acting for many students.

Photographs of student actors were taken at Sandy Spring Friends School, Sandy Spring, Maryland, by Peter Kline, instructor.

Paul Kozelka

INTRODUCTION

When I was a boy, we had dramatics. There was the school play, the Christmas pageant, the annual talent night to raise money for the volunteer firemen. With this enormous display complete, the old town could sit glowingly upon its talents while it waited for the circus to march into town. Drama was to dress up, to show off, and to parade.

Later, as a young teacher, I learned from one of my colleagues that all the arts were therapeutic, and I watched children finger painting and students "expressing themselves," but it was still very cheap art. Only lately have I seen teachers who see that art has meaning and that man's participating in it is the very record of his life. Teachers are beginning to realize that art is both a part and a shadow of life, and drama, the most moving of all the arts, is sometimes for an important show; but even more, the substance of our efforts to learn about the moving passions of life.

Peter Kline is uniquely qualified to present this book. He is a successful producer of outstanding performances both for adults and for high-school students, and he has that unique sense of self-involvement that pours passion into the struggling performance of a single child before an assembly audience. He has a rare capacity to see the part that the individual needs without needing to decide whether it is for show, for therapy, or for meaning. I cannot say whether he is a director, a teacher, a playwright, or an actor. He must be all of these. I know only that when his students make even their first halting steps, he is conscious of their needs and intensely aware of their growth. I suspect that part of his strength is his sensitive deliberation about words. A play is a group of words enslaved by the illusions that are created by those words. It is best served by an apt sense of clarity not only in the use of the words, but in the subservience of all the actions of the stage to the moving image that presents itself. If only modern people could realize that the image doesn't really exist! It is the words that are the substance of the presentation.

We have done so much to increase the importance of education in our society, and yet we have enfeebled it by failing to realize that it is not enough for us to gain the will to win the prize and the intellect to control it. Men, to be balanced and sensible, must also train their feelings, not for any picayune, playful goal of amusement and recreation, but because this is the very substance of unity in the design of a human soul. We are slow to comprehend that art is the primary record of our existence. The bison on the caveman's wall, the urn at the bottom of the sea, the ancient sphinx or the primitive record of an Incan weaver—all testify to our really comprehending each other only in terms of style and design.

Of all the arts, drama haunts us most with ourselves. It speaks of men and women and rests in the great illusion that their problems are important. We do not seek in *Hamlet* the answer to a philosophical question but the cracking of a noble heart. Some of us renew nobility in the midst of hesitation and cowardice; some renew the sense of beauty in a blind, deaf world; some seek to share the weight of noble leadership. Whether or not we find a timeless dignity in the waiting on death, we are made human with understanding.

All impulses are innocent in isolation, but drama and life itself are never isolated. Drama, the pretended action of life, remains our best means of seeing and feeling the life about us. We need its wisdom and its essential faith that life in full action is understood. Without the wisdom our direction would be lacking, and without the faith our lack of isolation would only prove us guilty.

John H. Burrowes
Headmaster
Friends School
Atlantic City, New Jersey

TO THE STUDENT

This book is designed to give you the kind of background information and interpretation that an experienced actor utilizes when preparing a role. The intention is that you consider carefully the meaning of every line and the expression of that meaning through the various resources available to the actor. If you work carefully on a few specific scenes, you will provide yourself with some of the experience necessary to approach an entire role effectively. It is hoped that from the book you will gain not so much specific points of interpretation as an attitude of careful questioning and the habit of careful weighing of each moment of a theatrical performance.

The demands that this book makes on you may seem formidable at first. Do not let that discourage you. Good acting is not done easily; it requires many years of careful study —and really great acting is achieved only by a few artists in each generation. You will be asked to do many things that are not easy for you, some that are impossible at first. But if you come back to these scenes repeatedly, you will find that they keep growing richer in your imagination. You should form the habit of making your reach exceed your grasp when you are trying to learn new things about acting. The actor who consistently attempts only those things that he can do easily soon becomes stilted and stereotyped, even if he is a star. The most exciting actors are those who are always seeking new challenges.

The interpretations in this book are presented in very specific terms, but that does not mean that there is anything necessary or final about them. A director of a production always makes certain that his interpretation is clear, but he may change it the next time he produces the same play. An actor may allow his interpretation of a scene to grow and change throughout his lifetime. Thus, there is no reason why you should not amend these interpretations according to your own feelings about the scenes. Any given performance, however, should be as specific as the interpretations we have provided. You should also seek every opportunity to see the scenes performed by others after you have mastered them yourself. You will learn that all performances differ and that the differences may be quite legitimate, though there are certainly both good and bad interpretations and performances.

Now for some general hints on how to approach each scene. Begin by reading the scene carefully and jotting down your impressions of it. You might ask yourself what sort of person you think is speaking. What are his objectives? What are his feelings about the things he says? Forming your own impression first will help you think about and react intelligently to the interpretation that follows.

Next, read the commentary on the play and the character. Think about each statement before you either accept it or reject it. Think about it both logically and emotionally. How does what is being said in the scene make you feel as a reader? How would it make you feel if you were the character? What is the emotional effect of the scene?

Next act out the scene according to the directions given. This will not be easy the first time. You will have to work through the scene many times until you are familiar enough with both the words and the stage directions to do it smoothly, even while reading it. Each time you do it, the scene will become clearer to you, no matter how well you have understood it before beginning to work on it. And as your performance improves, your enjoyment should increase correspondingly. You are really getting somewhere with the scene if you find that you don't want to stop working on it.

Now go on to study the comments on vocal and physical interpretation. This will enable you to polish the scene and move it in the direction of the external qualities of the character intended by the author. It is a good idea to develop these qualities before making your final judgments about the character's emotional outlook. People's emotional responses are shaped by their physical being. For example, a person with good posture and highly coordinated movement is likely to have emotions that are more focused, and, in a sense, more positive, than a poorly coordinated person. Thus, changing your posture can help you get emotional effects that would be very difficult otherwise.

Once the character feels right to you in an external sense, explore him more fully internally. Do some reading and thinking about him. You should read the entire work from which the selection is taken, looking for clues that will enrich the notions you have already developed. You may want to do some background reading about the character's time in history or the kind of problem he faces as a person, to help you clarify his feelings even further. You should also observe the behavior of as many different kinds of people as you can. Here and there you will find behavioral or postural characteristics that you can make use of in the character you are building.

You may gain additional insights by improvising scenes similar to the one you are working on. When improvising, try to recall experiences from your own life that are like the experiences you are enacting, and recreate in your imagination the emotions you felt at the time.

After you have by such means enriched your notion of the character (preferably while not working on the scene directly), return to the scene and repeat it many times, first exploring it in order to incorporate into it the new discoveries you have made and any inspirations you may have at the time, then letting it "set" into an interpretation that can be repeated many times in the same way and with the same effect.

You will probably become aware of conflicting elements in your performance: for example, vocal qualities that do not match physical qualities, or inflection patterns that do not seem to represent the emotions you have in mind. These conflicts may take some time to work out, and you should not try to resolve them too quickly. Part of the process must be unconscious: an integration of many disparate elements into a complex pattern. Some of this may occur during weeks or months when you do not work on the scene at all.

Finally, remember that although all good actors do many parts that they rehearse quickly and perform for only a short time without ever coming back to them, they also have some roles to which they return many times, whether in the theatre or in the imagination. You should have a few repertory pieces always on tap that you can perform whenever desirable and that you continue to reconsider throughout your lifetime as your acting matures. These will set a standard of performance for you that you will try to meet when performing other roles.

A few general remarks about acting may be helpful. Pay particular attention to the development of your voice. Properly supported tone originating from the diaphragm, not the larynx, diction clear enough to make the words sound effective at a considerable distance, and voice placement flexible enough to be adaptable to a number of different qualities of character, should all be developed early. Four basic vocal qualities are referred to from time to time in the text. A high, light quality, suggesting a naïve, innocent personality, is achieved by placing the voice as high as possible in the head. You should feel almost as if you were talking through your eyes. Most of the time you will use a voice that is centered in the face, warm and mature-sounding. If your voice seems to be projecting from about the level of your cheeks, you have placed it properly for this tone. For moments of grief or intimacy, or, sometimes, to indicate age, the voice will not be lifted much above the level of the throat. To indicate great strength a chest tone may be used. This tone should resonate in the chest and feel as if it is moving directly forward from it. Usually it is most effective when the voice is very low in pitch.

Because of the acoustical properties of your head, your voice does not sound the same to you as it does to others. In order to become familiar with the sound of your own voice, you should work with a tape recorder, or, failing that, stand facing a corner so that the sound is reflected back into your ears. You should become aware of what kind of sound you are making, so that you know what you are doing when you try to improve it. But don't become so self-conscious that you listen to the sound of your voice at the expense of attending to the total effect of the performance of which you are a part.

Physical control is as important for the actor as vocal control. The most common failing in beginners is a shifting of their weight back and forth at random while they are performing. Get yourself a brick and a board, place the board across the brick, and try to balance on it. When you can get through a whole speech without tipping the board, you have shown you are capable of balancing yourself properly while performing.

Very subtle changes in posture can have a tremendous effect on characterization. The actor who slouches while trying to play Hamlet cannot be successful in the role no matter how effective he is otherwise. Posture that is too rigid is not effective either. In general, you should assume a slightly different posture for each character you play, and that posture should reflect and intensify your feeling about the character.

Do not allow the chest to collapse so that there is too little room for air in your lungs, even if you are playing a cripple. You can hunch your shoulders while still keeping your chest cavity expanded. Also, unless you are playing a cripple, act from the center of your body, not one side or the other. Pretend that there is a light bulb in your solar plexus, and that everything about the character is unified as a result of coming from that one source. Do not allow one shoulder or hip to dominate your movement, but feel as if your whole body is equally involved in what is happening.

Remember that what you are doing is for the benefit of an audience. You must project every nuance, every gesture, every feeling for a considerable distance. Acting is in this sense larger than life. If you are not accustomed to projecting, it will feel awkward to you for a time. Everything you say and do will seem too big and unlike yourself. This feeling will disappear with practice.

It may not be easy for you to explore for the first time a character whose behavior patterns are very unlike your own. You may not like the sound of your voice or the movement of your body when they are doing unaccustomed things, no matter how effective they may actually be. You will get over this difficulty, though, after you have had some experience. Don't be afraid of acting badly at first. Many good actors start out by overacting terribly. Your mistakes will help to teach you what is *really* effective. Too many beginners get discouraged because they think they are not performing as well as they should. Good performances usually come only after a great deal of work, and many a mediocre actor turns into a good one as a result of strong motivation and a great deal of practice. Indeed, many actors who have become stars have recounted histories of early performances in which they acted badly. For one such example, see the remarks on Colley Cibber in the section on Lord Foppington.

There are many good actors who do not think, or think very little. But the best actors are usually careful students of the author's intentions. They believe it is very important to think through all the implications of a role in great detail. That means knowing what a character has been like before his part in the play begins, knowing what he does during the time he is offstage, and even knowing what his feelings are about many things that are not discussed in the play. It takes imagination and experience to reason correctly about such things, but even the beginner should try. An interesting exercise might be to read *Hamlet* and see how many things you can say about the characters of Rosencrantz and Guildenstern, whose parts are quite small. After you have thought carefully about them, read the play *Rosencrantz and Guildenstern Are Dead* by Tom Stoppard, and compare your impressions with the ones developed in that play. It portrays what might have happened to Rosencrantz and Guildenstern during the time they are not onstage in *Hamlet*. The characters have been elaborated considerably and in some ways fantastically by Stoppard, and much of the play requires careful reading to understand, but the sort of thinking Stoppard has done about these characters is the very sort that can be useful to an actor in enriching his characterization.

One final remark. You will need to know the areas of a stage in order to follow the stage directions in this book. Below is a diagram of the stage floor with the areas indicated. The abbreviations are: center (C), right (R), left (L), up (U), down (D). The terms "up" and "down" are used instead of "front" and "back" because in the early days of proscenium stages (that is, stages with curtains that can be pulled in front of the scene) the stage was slightly sloped upward away from the audience.

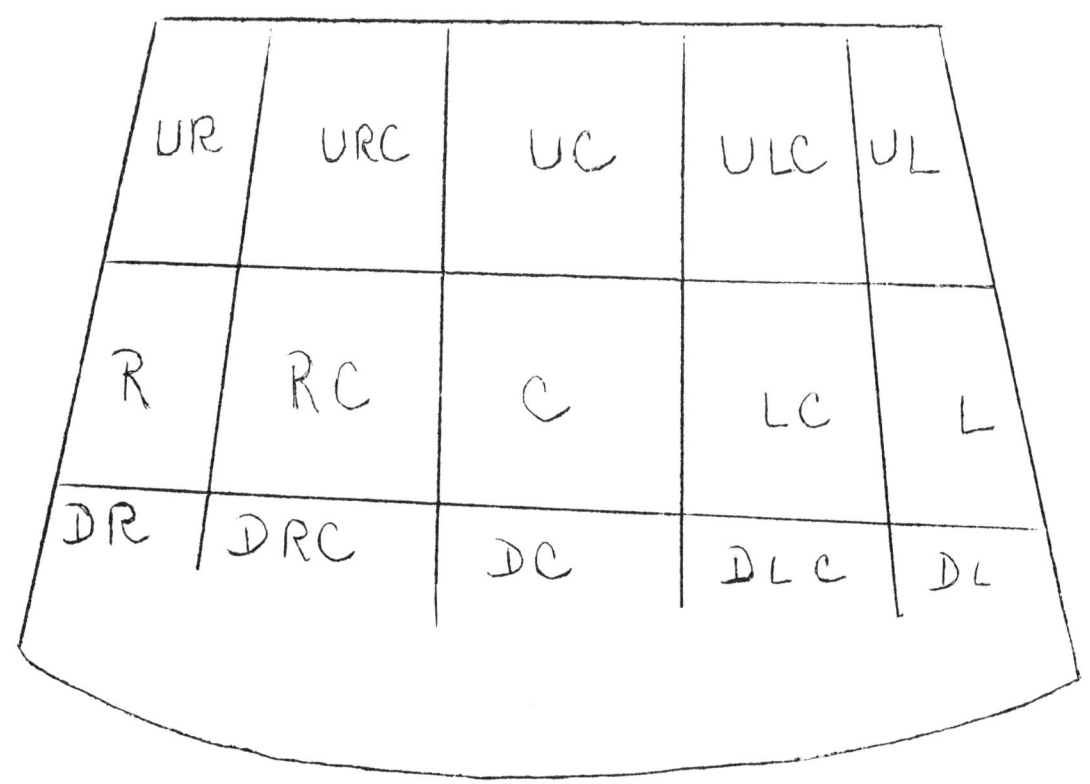

UR	URC	UC	ULC	UL
R	RC	C	LC	L
DR	DRC	DC	DLC	DL

TO THE TEACHER

I have selected the scenes in this book after working with them—and others like them—with high-school and college students over a period of ten years. They offer the student many different styles of playwriting from which to learn a wide range of acting techniques. Shakespeare is, of course, given a high proportion of space because of the value of repeated exposure to his work in developing acting ability. Though it has obviously been impossible to give a representative selection from world drama within one volume, there should be enough variety here to provide the student with an awareness of what kind of thinking is necessary in the preparation of almost any type of scene.

All of these scenes are monologues, although some may be staged with additional students reacting to the one who is speaking—in order to help him relate his performance to the responses of a silent companion, as well as to give students the idea that acting takes place while one is not speaking just as much as while one is. No dialogue scenes have been included because it is not always feasible to have students work together outside of class, and they can learn a great deal while working on their own. The instructor may wish to select other scenes from the same plays and have students work together in class once they have thought through some of the characterizations given here.

All the students in a class might be assigned the task of mastering a specified number of scenes in the book before going on to others that are not included here. If individuals do not study the scenes in the same order, there can be variety of performance within each class period, while students will also have the chance eventually to see others working on the same material they have worked on. If students are allowed to participate in the process of evaluating one another's work, they may become more critical of their own work. When a number of students have all thought through the same scene, the amount of critical awareness that may develop can be very impressive.

I have placed the selections in chronological order so as to suggest how language, theme, and characterization changed from the early Renaissance to the 19th century. The *Everyman* selection is included in order to give boys a chance to concentrate on the development of pure speech, something that does not come easily to most of them. The speech from *The Two Noble Kinsmen* has been included to give girls a chance to indulge in the kind of "ham" acting that does not come easily to many of them. The other scenes are largely self-explanatory. They are mostly "character" as opposed to "straight" roles, and mostly serious. This is because students seem to learn most easily and quickly from such selections. The skillful timing vital to much comedy is perhaps best approached after one has been successful a number of times in moving audiences emotionally. Boys can begin to develop a sense of timing working with Lord Foppington, and girls with Mabel Chiltern. Both of these scenes are funny enough in themselves so that they will usually delight audiences even when the performances are not very skillful.

Straight roles have been avoided because students are most comfortable when working with a characterization that does not depend too heavily on their own personality. As they become more advanced they will be better able to give convincing performances of characters that are much like themselves. Difficulties, however, have not been avoided, and the teacher should help the student evaluate just how fully developed a characterization it is appropriate for him to achieve at a given time. I have found that students in an acting class seldom need to polish their work to the performance level. Experience with a variety of different kinds of roles is valuable, even though the roles are not well suited to the personality of the actor. When a scene is undertaken as an exercise, in order to introduce a new dimension into the actor's range, it may not be necessary to polish it. Also, it is often wise to put a scene aside for a while, and come back to it when one has, through other kinds of experience, been able to achieve a new slant on it. From the point of view of performance, I have attempted to provide selections and suggestions that will challenge the most talented students, realizing that less talented ones will gain a great deal from achieving as much of what is suggested as they are capable of.

Some of the selections may be familiar to the students from their literature courses. Others will almost certainly be unfamiliar. Every student enjoys seeing some things he has already studied in literature courses, but also enjoys the novelty of exploring authors or plays he has not previously heard of.

Some scenes have been included that are not drama but make excellent acting exercises. This is done for the sake of greater literary richness, and to demonstrate the close relationship between theatre and other literary forms. These selections are ones students love to work on and that prove exceedingly actable.

A few notes on classroom technique may be helpful. I have found that in a class of from five to fifteen students meeting once or twice a week it is possible to do very productive teaching by devoting from five to fifteen minutes to each performance. The student performs the scene completely, and then the teacher asks the class for comments. After he has heard several reactions to his performance the student is eager to know what he can do to improve its weaknesses. That is when he turns expectantly to the instructor for suggestions. I usually suggest that he work on from one to four areas of his performance. I might, for example, suggest that he work for a week or two on improving his diction, breath control, and vocal quality. Or I might ask him to think through the motivations of his character on a line-by-line basis and (quite another area of concern) make some changes in the way he walks about the stage. A few specific exercises usually get far better results than more general statements, and, of course, positive comments are better than negative ones. The student needs to be told what he is doing right and to learn to build on that as a foundation.

Though only a third to a half of the class may perform during a given class period, all become deeply involved, since all can learn from seeing and thinking about the strengths and weaknesses of their classmates. In order to encourage such thinking, it is sometimes wise to point out similarities between approaches by different students. If a student realizes he has the same problem as one or more of his classmates, he will have a good idea of what its effect is in performance.

Most drama students are highly motivated, but often it is difficult for them to stand before their classmates the first few times. There will sometimes be a good deal of apologizing for what has been accomplished, and a tendency to feel that it is impossible to do what the teacher is asking. At such times it is good to be able to point to a student who has previously expressed hesitancy but has been successful. Often beginners feel that they cannot possibly do as well as their classmates are doing. Such feelings should be aired and discussed. It is reassuring for a beginner to feel that his doubts are shared by others. If a student is extremely reluctant to perform, it is a good idea to give him something simple enough to work on that he is certain of success with it. It may even be wise to work with him alone a few times in order to build his confidence. Don't force a student to do publicly what he feels very uncomfortable with—he may never want to act again. On the other hand, don't put up with too much laziness. If a student claims that he has not done his homework on a piece, I make him perform anyway. I usually find that he has been thinking about what I have told him, even if only unconsciously, and that it is possible for me to change my recommendations for him somewhat.

There doesn't seem to be any particular length of time a student should spend on a given scene. On occasion, one or two weeks may be enough, but I have often had students working on the same scene for months. The amount of time a student spends on a particular scene doesn't seem to be related to how well he is doing in the class. It is much more related to the kind of changes that are taking place in his acting. He may be so weak that he needs a great deal of repetition, or so good that he can approach a given scene in a large number of ways and still keep learning from it. On the average, I have found that a student will work on a particular scene for about a month or six weeks.

Finally, I should say that I have found teaching drama can be one of the most exciting ways in which to provide a deep and lasting educational experience. Because even students who are not highly motivated in many of their other classes will often show outstanding motivation in the study of drama, and because they can be taught individually and provided in a very short time with instructions for extended and meaningful activity outside the classroom, the drama teacher can accomplish a great deal, even when attendance is voluntary and the program is extracurricular.

The Theatre Student
SCENES TO PERFORM

EVERYMAN'S PRAYER

(from the morality play *Everyman*)

O eternal God, O heavenly figure,
O way of rightwiseness, O goodly vision,
Which descended down in a virgin pure
Because he would Everyman redeem,
Which Adam forfeited by his disobedience;
O blessèd Godhead, elect and high divine,
Forgive my grievous offence;
Here I cry thee mercy in this presence.
O ghostly treasure, O ransomer and redeemer
Of all the world, hope and conductor,
Mirror of joy, and founder of mercy,
Which illumineth heaven and earth thereby,
Hear my clamorous complaint, though it late be.
Receive my prayers; unworthy in this heavy life
Though I be, a sinner most abominable,
Yet let my name be written in Moses' table.
O Mary, pray to the Maker of all thing,
Me for to help at my ending,
And save me from the power of my enemy,
For death assaileth me strongly.
And, Lady, that I may by means of thy prayer
Of your Son's glory to be partaker,
By means of his passion I it crave;
I beseech you, help my soul to save.
Knowledge, give me the scourge of penance.
My flesh therewith shall give a quittance.
I will now begin, if God give me grace.

COMMENTARY

THE PLAY

Everyman is a morality play dating from the 15th century. It is the sort of play that Marlowe and Shakespeare probably saw when they were children, and that had a significant influence on their development. It is different from their plays, however, in a very important way. Its purpose is to represent and celebrate the glory of God, not to represent the world as it is perceived by the people in it. Consequently, while Shakespeare's characters think in terms of images or representations of sense experience, the characters in *Everyman* think only in terms of the mystical realities of religious experience.

To live at the time this play was written was to believe in God and the Kingdom of Heaven as the center of all life's meaning. The people of the Middle Ages and early Renaissance had a kind of certainty in their lives that we can never know. Everything they did and thought was related to this central reality. Consequently their thinking and behavior were, in a moral sense, beautifully and intricately organized. It was, by our standards, relatively easy for them to decide on the meaning and value of a thing or experience. That is why *Everyman* is written in such a simple, almost naïve style. Its simplicity has great strength, and the actor will have to find that strength before he can make the character convincing.

Everyman is an allegory. That is, the characters in it represent abstract ideas, and the action of which they are a part is not an action that could really take place. It is, rather, symbolic. It represents the significance of the life of a Christian, rather than its day-to-day reality. Everyman stands for all those people who have allowed their lives to proceed without specific concern for Christian moral issues. Most of the other characters represent facets of Everyman's life. The action is Everyman's attempt to enter the Kingdom of Heaven.

In the beginning of the play, God calls Death before him and announces that Everyman must be taken on a pilgrimage to decide whether or not he is worthy of Heaven. Everyman, who has not been expecting Death, tries to find among his companions those who will help him in his need. Fellowship, Kindred, Cousin, and Goods all desert him, and Good Deeds is too weak to help him. It is Knowledge who first assists Everyman with the famous words, "Everyman, I will go with thee, and be thy guide, in thy most need to go by thy side." Beauty, Strength, Discretion, and Five Wits then lend their assistance, and Everyman achieves his salvation.

THE CHARACTER

Since Everyman is not a real person, but an abstraction, it is necessary that he be played as simply as possible. Two things primarily characterize him: terror and faith. Everyman experiences terror when told he is going to die. This terror is much greater for him than it would be for a person living in our time, for it is a threat of death of the spirit and eternal suffering in Hell. Unless he can find salvation, Everyman is in the gravest danger. In another way, though, the terror is less frightening than a modern person's would be, for there is the definite possibility of salvation. Everyman's faith grows as this possibility becomes clearer to him.

THE SCENE

This scene occurs just after Knowledge has told Everyman that he must do penance for his sins. It is a simple prayer for forgiveness. In it we see the blossoming of Everyman's faith as he realizes that even though he is "a sinner and most abominable," he can achieve God's forgiveness.

The elaborate address to God with which the speech begins might seem a little artificial by our standards. But remember that Everyman's faith is based on his growing sense of the reality of God, and that reality is based on a number of manifestations. As Everyman speaks these opening lines he is feeling a much deeper sense of that reality than the words can possibly convey. God is eternal—that is, He lasts forever, transcends time, contains in Himself not only the present, but the past and future as well, all simultaneously, all as if they were a single moment. Consequently, God knows all about Everyman: what has happened to him, and what will happen to him. God is a heavenly figure. That is, He offers the promise of eternal life. God is the way of rightwiseness. That is, all moral questions are decided according to God's law, and through an understanding of that law one can resolve all questions of right and wrong. This is a source of strength and simplicity for Everyman. Once he has discovered God's law, he can be sure that all the powers of good are behind him, and he need never be troubled by doubt. God is a good vision. That is, He is something seen or thought of directly, not a mere abstraction. He is a person to whom Everyman can speak, and who will have a personal understanding of Everyman.

In the next three lines, Everyman refers to the drama of Adam's fall and Christ's redemption of man. Adam, having disobeyed the command of God, was cast out of Paradise, and from that time men were condemned to commit sin and suffer for it in Hell. It was only after God took upon Himself the actual suffering of humanity and was crucified that Paradise could again be offered to man. God's infinite mercy and grace were shown in the fact that He was willing to suffer in this way and restore salvation to men. This infinite mercy is intensely real to Everyman, for to him God is a person who suffered for him just as he himself might suffer. Throughout the prayer he is very much aware that God is going to give him far more than he deserves. He is deeply grateful to God, and humble before Him.

Having addressed God formally, Everyman makes his request: "Forgive my grievous offence." Everyman thinks of himself as sinful. He does not try to excuse or rationalize his sin in any way, as he might do if he were living in our time. To him it seems wonderful that God can be so much greater than he, and part of God's wonderfulness is that He *can* forgive Everyman's sin. And what is that sin? It is the sin of separation from God and His ways. While he was engrossed in worldly things, Everyman temporarily forgot that the world was created by God and had no meaning without God's laws. He lived according to his own pleasure, not God's.

Here is where the modern actor will have the greatest difficulty. It is part of our culture to feel that we can justify ourselves one way or another, and that through self-justification we receive salvation. Religious people justify themselves by good deeds, nonreligious people by doing those things they believe are most important. We tend to believe that people who are corrupt are so because of circumstances in their lives over which they had no control. They are "more to be pitied than censured." To think of ourselves as so deeply guilty that only an act of tremendous magnanimity by a Being infinitely greater than ourselves can redeem us is not part of our culture, even though occasionally it may be an individual's personal belief. Therefore, it is hard for a modern actor to speak from the heart without irony when he asks forgiveness for an offense that is his whole life. But that is just what Everyman is doing. His world contains many sinners for whom there can be no forgiveness, no redemption; people corrupted by Hell's influence, and committed to the service of the Devil. Simply not to be one of them is the greatest luxury he can think of, and he may escape from their number only through God's grace.

In the next few lines, Everyman's words are filled with deep love. His love of God is personal and direct. A woman speaking to a man whom she loved completely might have something of this same attitude if she felt her personality totally absorbed in his, if she felt that he alone could protect her from the dangers of the world. This is a love that submits oneself rather than striving to protect another. It is a love that can achieve fulfillment only through complete loss of oneself in something greater than oneself. Consequently there is something passive about it: it is not a reaching out with love, but a receiving of love into oneself. One might get some idea of the physical difference between the two kinds of love by comparing the act of hitting a baseball with a bat with the act of catching a baseball in a glove. The one requires firm aggressive action, the other awareness and readiness to receive. In one case one strikes at the ball, in the other case one allows one's hand to move backward with the ball. Therefore, Everyman will not shout at God: "I cry thee mercy," but will rather speak softly and gently, but with firm conviction. He will not become helplessly limp; he will become firmly ready to receive and benefit from the mercy he has asked for.

God is a "ghostly," a spiritual, treasure. Sometimes religious experience is symbolized by the transfixing quality of a beautiful jewel. If you have ever looked at such a thing and momentarily allowed its beauty to absorb your whole attention so that you have lost your awareness of everything else, you have some idea of what Everyman is talking about here. To him, God is literally a "treasure," something he loves, something that transfixes him and makes everything else seem unimportant. This feeling of God's beauty is given greater force by the knowledge that He is ransomer and redeemer of all the world. Everything in the world that is not part of God's kingdom is worthless or corrupt. Everyman senses that all truly beautiful things have their beauty because of God, and that this beauty is now entering his soul. All hope for eternal joy is to be found in God, who also through His laws conducts one toward that joy. That joy is entirely reflected in His face, as all beautiful things point toward Him. God's mercy, so closely linked in Everyman's mind with beauty, becomes at last a kind of shining light illuminating all of heaven and earth.

When he thinks of the greatness of God's beauty, Everyman's terror at the possibility of losing that beauty suddenly increases. He realizes how late in his life he has come to desire Heaven, and he raises a great cry ("clamorous complaint") at his own misfortune. He begs to have his name written in Moses' tablet, which he considers a symbol of penance. He begs for this, even though he realizes he is "unworthy in this heavy life, a sinner most abominable." Looking back over his past actions, he can hardly imagine having done such terrible things, and therefore speaks of himself as a sinner most abominable and thinks of his life as "heavy," something that weighs him down from the exhilarating joy that God holds out to him.

Feeling for a moment that his sin is too great to allow him to speak to God directly, he turns to the Virgin Mary, mother of Christ, and asks her to intercede for him, just as a child who has done wrong might go to his mother and ask her to persuade his father not to punish him too harshly.

Having realized how dangerous his sinful ways have been, he thinks of the temptations of the Devil, temptations to which he had previously succumbed, as terribly threatening, and it seems to him that the Devil is his personal enemy, much in the same way that God is his personal friend.

Having identified Mary as protection from his enemy, he grows even warmer toward her, believing also in her power to help him in a more positive way. Because Christ died on the cross for mankind (this was His "passion"), it is possible for Everyman to share in His glory, which is the glory of Heaven, provided only that Mary will intercede for him because she believes him to be worthy of salvation.

Believing now that he can achieve salvation because he has affirmed his faith in God's mercy, Everyman proceeds to do what will be necessary to achieve salvation. He turns to his friend Knowledge, who has promised to help him, and asks her to tell what he must do as penance to drive evil from himself. His flesh will give quittance; that is, he will pay whatever penalty he must through physical suffering. Having assured himself that he knows what to do and that he is willing to do it, he speaks with great determination and joy.

Simple as this scene is in its expression of terror and faith, it is one of the most beautiful and powerful scenes that one can find anywhere in the literature of drama. Every great hero is moved by a cause that strikes to the core of his being. Every hero knows how to love, hate, and fear in important ways. But probably no hero is so profoundly moved by all the important issues of life as Everyman is in this scene.

The fact that few of us can feel the kind of relationship with God that Everyman feels, if only because we live at a different time in history, does not mean that Everyman's feelings are irrelevant or that they cannot be the subject of great drama. It is not necessary for the actor to accept Everyman's beliefs as his own in order to act the part. It is only necessary for him to understand what they are and believe that they are feelings that make sense for Everyman.

EVERYMAN'S PRAYER

(*Everyman stands in the center of the stage. Next to him is Knowledge, who has just told him that he must fulfill his penance. Everyman kneels, his head bowed, his hands in an attitude of prayer.*)

O eternal God, O heavenly figure,
O way of rightwiseness, O goodly vision,
Which descended down in a virgin pure
Because he would Everyman redeem,
Which Adam forfeited by his disobedience.

(*He raises his head, looking up to God.*)

O blesséd Godhead, elect and high divine,

(*He stretches out his arms toward Heaven.*)

Forgive my grievous offence;
Here I cry thee mercy in this presence.

(*He draws his hands back down to his chest, the fingers of one hand cupping the knuckles of the other. As he speaks, the passion of his feeling is shown by a slight waving of the head on the important words.*)

O ghostly treasure, O ransomer and redeemer
Of all the world, hope and conductor,
Mirror of joy, and founder of mercy,
Which illumineth heaven and earth thereby,

(*He drops his head, closing his eyes, feeling the depth of his plight. The word "late" has great heaviness. There is a long pause at the end of the line.*)

Hear my clamorous complaint, though it late be.

(*A sharp intake of breath indicates the pain of this next plea. He raises his head sharply and almost cries out, but manages to keep the tone restrained.*

Jesse Barber as Everyman:
"Forgive my grievous offence;
 Here I cry thee mercy in this presence."

After the first phrase, his speech gathers momentum for two and a half lines, as if he is rushing to get to the point of his plea.)

> Receive my prayers; unworthy in this heavy life
> Though I be, a sinner most abominable,
> Yet let my name be written in Moses' table.

(He looks to the right and slightly lower, addressing Mary.)

> O Mary, pray to the Maker of all thing,
> Me for to help at my ending,
> And save me from the power of my enemy,
> For death assaileth me strongly.

(The right hand is extended slightly out, the elbow bent, the palm up, the fingers curved and close together.)

> And, Lady, that I may by means of thy prayer
> Of your Son's glory to be partaker,
> By means of his passion I it crave;[1]
> I beseech you, help my soul to save.

(He rises, and faces Knowledge.)

> Knowledge, give me the scourge[2] of penance.
> My flesh therewith shall give a quittance.
> I will now begin, if God give me grace.

NOTES

[1] "And, Lady, I crave that, by means of your prayer, I may partake of your Son's glory which he gave me the opportunity to do by His suffering on the cross."

[2] *scourge*, whip. Everyman will use this to flay his body as penance for his sin. This is because the body, merely because it is physical and among the things of the earth, is associated with sin. In some editions Everyman has been given the scourge by Confession before he begins his prayer. In others, Confession gives it to Knowledge, who holds it during the prayer. Thus the actor may decide whether he wishes to hold the whip in this scene or whether he wishes to reach out his hand to Knowledge to take it at this time. If he wishes, he may do neither, interpreting the request as one for moral support, rather than for the physical object, and assuming that Knowledge will give him the whip a moment later during her own speech.

VOCAL AND PHYSICAL CHARACTERIZATION

As soon as Leo left, I turned to the cat. It makes no difference what position I invent for him, whether he is put down head first, or made to lie on his side or back. He hangs by each of his paws in succession and all four at once. Each time it is easy to see that he bends like a spring for a second, and then, with extraordinary ease, arranges his muscles, loosening up those he does not need, and holding tense the ones he is using. What amazing adaptability!*

So writes the great teacher of acting, Constantin Stanislavski, about the problem of muscular relaxation. People living in our age

---
* Constantin Stanislavski, *An Actor Prepares*. Translated by Elizabeth Reynolds Hapgood. (New York: Theatre Arts Books, 1936), p. 97.

have great difficulty achieving the kind of behavior described above. They are at war with themselves in many different ways, and their conflicts are reflected in muscular tensions throughout the body.

A man who is capable of the deep and abiding faith in God that Everyman expresses in the passage we are considering is troubled only by a single conflict: the conflict in his own character between good and evil. The complexities and side issues with which we are familiar are foreign to his experience. As a result, he will move with the kind of singleness of purpose that characterizes the cat. His whole body is completely relaxed, except that part he is using at a particular moment. His actions are simple and graceful. His whole being is concentrated in each gesture, and nothing is held back. Such simplicity and grace (not the grace of a ballet dancer, but the grace of a farmer accustomed to conserving his energies so that he may accomplish as much work as possible) are very difficult to achieve, but they are essential to make the audience believe in the absolute nature of Everyman's faith.

Good posture is essential. The head must be held so that the spinal column is straight all the way down. Stand against a wall with the head, shoulders, and heels touching it, and try to preserve that erectness of posture as you move. As you walk, try to feel the motion of walking equally distributed throughout your legs. Let the ankles and knees absorb the shock of your feet hitting the ground enough so that you do not bounce up and down as you move. If you gesture with your arm, use the whole arm, and make the gesture large, clear, and complete. That is, move your arm from one comfortable position to another. If you turn, let the upper and lower parts of your body work together. Do not allow your arms to point in one direction, your feet in another. All these things should help you create the impression of a man who is totally committed spiritually, mentally, and physically to the action he has decided to take.

Because he is an abstraction, not a particular human being, Everyman's voice should have power but no character. It should be as pure a sound as the actor can produce, without mannerisms of any kind. The tone should be supported from the diaphragm and should resonate in the chest and be centered in the middle of the face. The voice should be neither too heavy nor too light, and should have no harshness, raspiness, or breathiness. Remember that the actor's job in this case is not to show the audience a particular person, but rather a relationship to God that all of them are asked to share. The less they identify the actor as a particular person, the more able they will be to see in him their own personal strivings.

THE DEATH OF ZENOCRATE

(from *Tamburlaine the Great, Second Part* by Christopher Marlowe)

Black is the beauty of the brightest day;
The golden ball of heaven's eternal fire,
That danc'd with glory on the silver waves,
Now wants the fuel that inflam'd his beams;
And all with faintness, and for foul disgrace,
He binds his temples with a frowning cloud,
Ready to darken earth with endless night.
Zenócrate, that gave him light and life,
Whose eyes shot fire from their ivory brows,
And temper'd every soul with lively heat,
Now by the malice of the angry skies,
Whose jealousy admits no second mate,
Draws in the comfort of her latest breath,
All dazzled with the hellish mists of death.
Now walk the angels on the walls of heaven,
As sentinels to warn th' immortal souls
To entertain divine Zenocrate:
Apollo, Cynthia, and the ceaseless lamps
That gently look'd upon this loathsome earth,
Shine downwards now no more, but deck the heavens
To entertain divine Zenocrate:
The crystal springs, whose taste illuminates
Refinéd eyes with an eternal sight,
Like triéd silver run through Paradise
To entertain divine Zenocrate:
The cherubins and holy seraphins,
That sing and play before the King of Kings,
Use all their voices and their instruments
To entertain divine Zenocrate;
And, in this sweet and curious harmony,
The god that tunes this music to our souls
Holds out his hand in highest majesty
To entertain divine Zenocrate.
Then let some holy trance convey my thoughts
Up to the palace of th' empyreal heaven,

That this my life may be as short to me
As are the days of sweet Zenocrate.

*   *   *   *   *   *   *   *

What, is she dead? Techélles, draw thy sword,
And wound the earth, that it may cleave in twain,
And we descend into th' infernal vaults,
To hale the Fatal Sisters by the hair,
And throw them in the triple moat of hell,
For taking hence my fair Zenocrate.
Casáne and Therídamus, to arms!
And with the cannon break the frame of heaven;
Batter the shining palace of the sun,
And shiver all the starry firmament,
For amorous Jove hath snatched my love from hence,
Meaning to make her stately queen of heaven.
What god soever holds thee in his arms,
Giving thee nectar and ambrosia,
Behold me here, divine Zenocrate,
Raving, impatient, desperate and mad,
And, if thou pitiest Tamburlaine the Great,
Come down from heaven, and live with me again.

COMMENTARY

THE PLAY

Christopher Marlowe was the first of the great Elizabethan dramatists, and it is thought by some that he was Shakespeare's chief instructor in playwriting. He was the inventor of what was called "Marlowe's mighty line," a line of blank verse that had unusual power both in imagery and in sound. An often quoted example of this type of line is Doctor Faustus' description of Helen of Troy, "Was this the face that launched a thousand ships?" You will find many other examples in the present selection.

Many of Marlowe's plays center around a hero who desires to transcend the limitations of human experience and live as a superman or a god. His play about Tamerlane, the 14th-century Mongol who set out to conquer the world and actually did subdue a sizable portion of the Middle East, was so popular that it was followed by a sequel. Today the two plays are sometimes shortened and performed as a single evening's entertainment.

Marlowe's Tamburlaine* has recklessly, almost breathlessly, conquered one kingdom after another and had his way in nearly everything he has desired; but there is one fact of life about which he can do nothing: death. His first great setback comes when he is faced with the fatal illness of his beloved Queen, Zenocrate. The scene we are concerned with is the one in which he stands by her deathbed and expresses his grief. You will find in his speech two poetic devices of importance: hyperbole, which is the use of greatly exaggerated metaphors to express intense emotion; and apostrophe, which is speech addressed to an absent person, a god, or an abstract idea as if it were present.

* Elizabethan spelling was seldom consistent with our own.

Tamburlaine uses apostrophe in the strictest sense only when he addresses the dead Zenocrate directly, but he so peoples the heavens with angels and gods that we have the feeling of apostrophe throughout the speech. Tamburlaine's sense of his own tremendous power is reflected in the fact that he feels the whole universe must share his sorrow. Such identification between the fates of great men and the forces of nature was quite common in Elizabethan thinking, and thus it seemed natural to Marlowe's audience that Tamburlaine should call upon the gods and forces of nature to entertain Zenocrate perpetually in Heaven.

The Character

The chief characteristics of Tamburlaine are power and ambition. These are characteristics of Richard III and Macbeth also, but unlike Shakespeare's villains, Marlowe's are not conniving and guilt-ridden; they are men of almost insuperable power who can glory in their supreme achievements while totally forgetting that what they are doing is evil. Tamburlaine never gives a second thought to the brutalities that he metes out to his enemies or tries to rationalize them in any way. Because he is superior in strength and intelligence to other men, it seems to follow that whatever he desires should be his. Such a man cannot be defeated by other men, only by God. Tamburlaine is not, like Shakespeare's characters, a believable human being; he is a creature of Marlowe's imagination, a creature who can exist only in the drama, and can give expression to man's unlimited aspirations. In many ways he is Richard III's opposite. He is direct where Richard is conniving. He is powerful and handsome, while Richard is deformed and ugly. He regards the world as his by right, whereas Richard thinks of it as something he must take because his rights have been denied him. He can love, deeply and genuinely, as Richard cannot. There is little if any irony in the character of Tamburlaine.

The secret of the poetry is in its energy and power, its naïve self-confidence. It would be easy to poke fun at Marlowe, to show that his characters cannot be real, that their aspirations are child-like. But one is not tempted to, because unreal as his characters are, Marlowe has with the mightiness of his poetry made us accept them.

Therefore the only reasonable approach to Marlowe is suspension of disbelief. That is, the actor must take everything the character says at face value and play it to the hilt. He must believe in Marlowe's characters as much as Marlowe does, and as he speaks the words of Tamburlaine it must for the moment seem to him possible that the gods really will behave like servants, arranging the heavens to suit his desires.

The Scene

To the lover it seems as if his loved one is responsible for all the beauty in the world. Romeo says of Juliet, "She doth teach the torches to burn bright," and later speaks of her as the sun: "Arise, fair sun, and kill the envious moon." Tamburlaine thinks of Zenocrate in exactly the same way. Now that she is dying, the sun, which gained its brightness from Zenocrate, must lose it. He does not capture the feeling in a few words, as Romeo does, but devotes several lines to it. The sun is personified. He has lost the fuel that inflamed his beams, and surrounds himself with clouds in disgrace at that loss. Never again, thinks Tamburlaine, will there be light in the world. The brightest day will be black in its beauty.

Why must Zenocrate die? Because the skies are jealous. They cannot allow anyone to rival the sun's brilliance. Therefore, she lies dying, breathing her latest breath, which paradoxically dazzles her toward darkness with the "hellish mists of death."

But though the skies may be jealous, those who populate them are not. The angels must walk about the walls of heaven warning the souls of the immortals to entertain

Zenocrate, who is divine, and therefore one of them. Tamburlaine's intensely visual imagination creates the scene for us; we almost feel that it has arisen at his command.

Who are the immortal souls that the angels must warn? They may be the souls of all those who have died and ascended into heaven. They may also be the souls of the Roman gods, some of whom are mentioned in the speech. It is common for Elizabethan characters to mix their Christianity with classical mythology, speaking in one breath of angels, in another of Apollo, Cynthia, and the like. This is not paganism; it is merely a reflection of the fact that the Elizabethan from his earliest days in school had studied the Bible and also the classical authors. It seemed natural to think of the universe as populated by both Christian and Roman figures, though most people took for granted that the Christian figures were real and the Roman ones were not. The point is that for Tamburlaine the world is not dominated by a single personal God as we might think of it, but rather by a supreme monarch of the skies with many angels and lesser divinities carrying out his commands. Just as England was ruled by a queen who was supreme, but whose authority was reflected in the work of innumerable public officers, so it seemed natural that God should operate in the same way.

Apollo, god of the sun, Cynthia, goddess of the moon, and the stars will shine on earth no more, for without Zenocrate it has become loathsome; they will rather confine their beauty to the heavens where she will reside. In Paradise, Zenocrate will also enjoy drinking from the crystal springs that will enable her to live forever by giving her eyes eternal sight.

Cherubins and Seraphins were the highest of the nine orders of angels in the heavenly hierarchy. They were therefore those who stood closest to the throne of God. Tamburlaine's suggestion that their songs in praise of God become entertainment for Zenocrate borders on the blasphemous and is another suggestion of the god-like proportions of his sense of greatness. The singing of the angels is no ordinary song: it is the music of the spheres, the heavenly harmony that gives the stars and planets an orderly pattern in their motions about the earth. By its means the laws of nature work smoothly. To disturb this music would be to threaten the return of Chaos, the original state of confusion out of which God created the universe, for it is a symbol of the order of all things in Creation. The God that tunes this music is therefore the King of Kings himself, and it is He who holds out His hand to Zenocrate, He too who will entertain her.

Tamburlaine, imagining the glorious reception Zenocrate has received in Heaven, desires that his thoughts be carried up to Heaven that God may know he too would like to die and share Zenocrate's happiness. But this is the Heaven of his imagination, a Heaven in which Zenocrate has taken a position of great prominence, and in which he himself would presumably do so as well. He has created for himself a position of centrality in the universe. In the process he threatens to alter its very order.

Why should Tamburlaine have such ambitions? The religious man of the Middle Ages could think of no greater happiness than taking his rightful place in Heaven, and no greater terror than being condemned to Hell. But Marlowe's Tamburlaine is a Renaissance man. For him there is confusion as to whether the eternal scheme of things is as it was once thought to be. Copernicus had suggested that the earth revolved around the sun, and was therefore not the center of the universe, and Copernicus was beginning to be taken seriously. Social conventions of the time dictated that one should seek promotion in court rather than merely attempt to gain a proper place in Heaven. Should man live for this world or the next? One way to react to such a problem was to doubt the meaning of all existence, to become an atheist and a cynic, to become ambitious as Richard III was, without thought of consequence. Another way was naïvely to ignore the problem, to assume that man could have the best of both worlds; and that is what Tamburlaine is doing. His apparent blasphemy then would appear not so much blasphemy as a child-like belief that he can somehow rise to the highest position in the universe, and that the relationship between himself and God is a close personal one in which he is naturally the central figure. In his flights of fancy, then, Tamburlaine really does have the best of both worlds.

But in reality, things are quite different. Zenocrate dies, and Tamburlaine is left alive and in grief for her. He calls on his companions, Techélles, Casáne, and Therídamus, to take action in response to his grief. A world that he has supposed would do whatever he commanded of it has earned his supreme anger when it disappoints him for the first time. The Fatal Sisters, three mythical women who spin out the thread of one's life and cut the thread to bring death, have become the objects of his desire for revenge. He commands that the world be cut in half so that he can descend into it and punish them for what they have done.

Now Tamburlaine sees the god whom a moment before he has imagined receiving his queen into heaven as a rival whom he must conquer. This time, however, it is not as the King of Kings that he thinks of him, but as the Roman deity, Jove. He wishes to fire his cannon against the god's palace and punish him for the crime of seducing his love.

Finally, Tamburlaine turns to Zenocrate herself (not the body that lies before him, but the spirit that now dwells in Heaven), and asks her to take pity on him, renounce whatever god is now wooing her, and come back to him. It is in this moment of realizing that she really is dead and no longer with him (emotionally accepting it now, though of course he has known the fact earlier) that he goes mad with grief, and that he hits the highest peak of emotion in the scene.

The charge was made against Christopher Marlowe during his lifetime that he was an atheist, and his mysterious death may have been somehow an outcome of this charge. It is easy to see from our selection how such an accusation might have been made, but not easy to determine whether it was correct. Marlowe himself may not have known, for he was a poet, not a thinker, and his poetry records the feelings he could imagine passing through the mind of a great hero, feelings he perhaps wished he might have been great enough to entertain himself. The important thing to observe is that Tamburlaine takes God very seriously even though he does not pay Him what we would consider due respect. Perhaps, after all, he does worship God in his own way, for God is the only being in the universe whom Tamburlaine is willing to take seriously and regard as a genuine rival. And Marlowe is showing us that Tamburlaine has entered a skirmish that he cannot possibly win.

THE DEATH OF ZENOCRATE

(Zenocrate is lying in her bed of state, LC. Tamburlaine sits near her, C. Three physicians are about her bed, administering medicine. Her three sons, Calyphas, Amyras, and Celebinus, stand DL. Therídamus, Techélles, and Usumcasáne, three kings who are followers of Tamburlaine, stand DR. Tamburlaine looks at Zenocrate, his left hand extended to her. One of the physicians shakes his head, indicating that there is little hope for Zenocrate. Tam-

burlaine clenches his left fist and bows his head. Tears come to his eyes. Then he looks up to the heavens.)

> Black is the beauty of the brightest day;
> The golden ball of heaven's eternal fire,
> That danc'd with glory on the silver waves,
> Now wants the fuel that inflam'd his beams;
> And all with faintness and for foul disgrace,
> He binds his temples with a frowning cloud,

(He bows his head again, the words coming slowly, bitterly.)

> Ready to darken earth with endless night.

(He looks at Zenocrate.)

> Zenócrate,

(His eyes flashing, he looks to the heavens, speaking angrily and quickly.)

> that gave him light and life,
> Whose eyes shot fire from their ivory brows,
> And temper'd every soul with lively heat,

(Rises, shaking his fist at the heavens.)

> Now by the malice of the angry skies,

(Fire in his voice on the word "jealousy.")

> Whose jealousy admits no second mate,

(He turns, extending his arm slowly toward Zenocrate. His voice becomes gentle and loving, though there is still an undertone of bitterness in it.)

> Draws in the comfort of her latest breath,

(His voice becomes very dark and heavy, and on the word "death" he closes his eyes and allows himself a moment of quiet grief.)

> All dazzled with the hellish mists of death.

(His arms are extended full length to heaven. His voice is like a trumpet. He is creating vividly in his imagination the scene he describes.)

> Now walk the angels on the walls of heaven,
> As sentinels to warn th' immortal souls

(Faces her, holding himself proudly erect, having turned his grief into a moment of triumph.)

> To entertain divine Zenocrate:

(Gestures with his right hand toward where the sun might be, with his left hand where the moon might be, and then with both hands takes in the full sweep of heaven, to indicate the stars.)

The Death of Zenocrate / 39

Peter Fredin as Tamburlaine:
"For amorous Jove hath snatched my love from hence,
Meaning to make her stately queen of heaven."

Apollo, Cynthia, and the ceaseless lamps
That gently look'd upon this loathsome earth,

(*Shakes his head slowly, his voice is commanding.*)

Shine downwards now no more,

(*His right hand reaches up to indicate the heavens; with his left hand again he indicates Zenocrate. These gestures have kingly grace.*)

                                         but deck the heavens
To entertain divine Zenocrate:

(*These next images are more gentle. Tamburlaine might hold his left hand palm up about the level of his waist. He should almost sing the words, very gently. His eyes may be closed as he imagines the scene, but they must open on "eternal sight."*)

The crystal springs, whose taste illuminates
Refinéd eyes with an eternal sight,
Like triéd silver run through Paradise
To entertain divine Zenocrate:

(*His voice becomes even gentler and more lilting. He seems to be listening to the music of the angels. Again, his eyes may be closed.*)

The cherubins and holy seraphins,
That sing and play before the King of Kings,
Use all their voices and their instruments
To entertain divine Zenocrate;

(*His voice grows more intense in its music. On "god" his right hand gestures toward heaven. On "holds out his hand" his left hand gestures toward Zenocrate.*)

And, in this sweet and curious harmony,
The god that tunes this music to our souls
Holds out his hand in highest majesty

(*He looks from Zenocrate to the direction in which his right hand points, as if to lift the spirit of Zenocrate into the heavens.*)

To entertain divine Zenocrate.

(*He slowly sits, his eyes closed. He speaks very softly and slowly, just above a whisper, trying to create in himself the trance of which he speaks. Sustaining the vowel sound in the word "sweet" will suggest the intensity of his emotion, the pure joy of his love which he has managed to distill out of the grief he now feels.*)

Then let some holy trance convey my thoughts
Up to the palace of th' empyreal heaven,
That this my life may be as short to me
As are the days of sweet Zenocrate.

        *   *   *   *   *   *   *   *

(*Tamburlaine asks one of the physicians how Zenocrate is, and he replies that she is about to undergo a terrible fit which she may not survive. Tamburlaine tells Zenocrate that if she dies it will kill him. She replies that she wishes to die and pleads with him not to spoil her desire for a second life in Heaven. She then asks for music and falls into a fit. While the music is playing, she dies.*)

* * * * * * * *

(*Tamburlaine rises, and steps back in disbelief. He is unable to comprehend as yet what has happened. His jaw drops, he gasps for breath; finally, he speaks in a quiet, broken voice.*)

What, is she dead?

(*He turns to Techélles, who stands DR, and speaks in a voice that gathers volume and momentum like an erupting volcano. His arm flies into the air and then gestures at the earth, pantomiming a sword.*)

    Techélles, draw thy sword,
And wound the earth, that it may cleave in twain,
And we descend into th' infernal vaults,
To hale the Fatal Sisters by the hair,
And throw them in the triple moat of hell,
For taking hence my fair Zenocrate.

(*A second explosion, more violent than the first, and rising to the limit of the actor's capacity for intensity. With both arms, Tamburlaine gestures threateningly at heaven.*)

  Casáne and Therídamus, to arms!
And with the cannon break the frame of heaven;
Batter the shining palace of the sun,
And shiver all the starry firmament,

(*Tamburlaine is exhausted from violence and grief. He speaks pitifully, and begins to weep.*)

  For amorous Jove hath snatched my love from hence,
Meaning to make her stately queen of heaven.

(*He falls to the ground weeping. When he has exhausted himself with tears, he raises his head slowly from the ground and speaks with a voice that has no more strength in it than a child's might. He feels completely helpless, and he is pleading desperately.*)

  What god soever holds thee in his arms,
Giving thee nectar and ambrosia,
Behold me here, divine Zenocrate,
Raving, impatient, desperate and mad,
And, if thou pitiest Tamburlaine the Great,
Come down from heaven, and live with me again.

VOCAL AND PHYSICAL CHARACTERIZATION

A deep, resonating chest tone will best capture the power and lack of introspection that characterize Tamburlaine. The actor should produce a tone that sings the poetry of the words, emphasizing, indeed sustaining, the vowel sounds.

Breath control must be very good, too. The actor must be able to sustain a phrase that is several lines long without giving the slightest suspicion of being short of breath.

Because the power in the speech is almost entirely on the surface (nothing is being suppressed), it is hard to avoid the effect of simply shouting one's way through it. There is little that can be said at less than full volume. The only way to combat such an effect is to approach each of the sentences (most of which are four to eight lines long) with a different kind of attack, reflecting the detailed changes of attitude the character is experiencing. Pause between the sections, and prepare for a new burst of energy, thinking carefully as you do so what modifications you will make in the energy itself.

Tamburlaine is both powerful and well coordinated. To radiate convincingly the power that characterizes him, one must imagine one's body to be heavier than it really is, but at the same time move with the greatest ease. Every part of the body must be energized and given weight. All gestures are very full and large, without any compromise. When Tamburlaine shakes his fist at heaven, his entire body is behind the gesture. When he falls to the ground weeping, he almost throws his whole body at the ground.

The actor must practice all physical movement and gesture until it is completely under control. Remember that the sort of hand-to-hand combat in which Tamburlaine excelled requires not only tremendous force but also incredible precision. If such a man were ever once off by a sixteenth of an inch in his aim, it might cost him his life. That kind of discipline has given Tamburlaine a beautiful gracefulness along with his strength. It is the grace of a tiger about to spring on his prey.

RICHARD ALONE

(from *Richard III* by William Shakespeare)

Now is the winter of our discontent
Made glorious summer by this sun of York;
And all the clouds that lowered upon our house
In the deep bosom of the ocean buried.
Now are our brows bound with victorious wreaths,
Our bruiséd arms hung up for monuments,
Our stern alarums changed to merry meetings,
Our dreadful marches to delightful measures.
Grim-visaged war hath smoothed his wrinkled front,
And now, instead of mounting barbéd steeds
To fright the souls of fearful adversaries,
He capers nimbly in a lady's chamber
To the lascivious pleasing of a lute.
But I, that am not shaped for sportive tricks
Nor made to court an amorous looking glass;
I, that am rudely stamped, and want love's majesty
To strut before a wanton ambling nymph;
I, that am cúrtailed of this fair proportion,
Cheated of feature by dissembling Nature,
Deformed, unfinished, sent before my time
Into this breathing world, scarce half made up,
And that so lamely and unfashionable
That dogs bark at me as I halt by them—
Why, I, in this weak piping time of peace,
Have no delight to pass away the time,
Unless to see my shadow in the sun
And descant on mine own deformity.
And therefore, since I cannot prove a lover
To entertain these fair well-spoken days,
I am determinéd to prove a villain
And hate the idle pleasures of these days.
Plots have I laid, inductions dangerous,
By drunken prophecies, libels, and dreams,
To set my brother Clarence and the King
In deadly hate the one against the other;

44 / Scenes to Perform

> And if King Edward be as true and just
> As I am subtle, false and treacherous,
> This day should Clarence closely be mewed up
> About a prophecy which says that G
> Of Edward's heirs the murderer shall be.
> Dive, thoughts, down to my soul: here Clarence comes!

COMMENTARY

THE PLAY

Richard III as characterized by Shakespeare is one of the greatest villains in history, although modern historical scholarship suggests that he was actually a rather good king. In the Wars of the Roses, which divided England from 1455 to 1484, that is, from the time of Henry VI to the ascension to the throne of Henry VII, the rival families of York and Lancaster were involved in many struggles for power against each other. Our play begins during a temporary lull in hostilities after supporters of the House of York have seized power and crowned Edward IV. Richard, Duke of Gloucester, is King Edward's younger brother. He wishes to become king, but cannot do so until those who stand between him and the throne have died. These are the King himself, two little princes (heirs to the throne), and Richard's elder brother, George, Duke of Clarence. Richard engineers the murders of Clarence, of the two princes, and of many others who have power in England. After the natural death of Edward, Richard ultimately becomes king, but his reign is troubled by his own tortured conscience and by the rebellion against him led by the Earl of Richmond, later to become Henry VII, first of the great Tudor monarchs and grandfather of Elizabeth, Shakespeare's own sovereign.

THE CHARACTER

To understand Richard III, one must know something of the Elizabethan attitude toward crime and guilt. The villain in a Shakespearean play is descended from the Vice, a character in the plays of the late Middle Ages, who was identified with the Devil in a religious sense, but who was frequently a comic character. He was assumed to be committed to evil, and to have neither a guilty conscience nor any desire to rationalize away his guilt by placing the blame for it on others. He enjoyed being evil, though he was almost certainly punished in the end, and went to his punishment naïvely asserting that it was fully deserved. On this partly comic, fully evil character type Shakespeare has superimposed his own understanding of human nature, so that Richard has something of medieval simplicity, something of modern psychology. He is no longer really comic, though he has many humorous moments and is meant to receive little sympathy from the audience. On the one hand, Richard admits his evil intentions, taking the audience fully into his confidence. On the other hand, he attempts to account for his evil character by pointing to the pathos of his situation in life: since he is deformed he cannot enjoy life as others do, and must find his satisfactions perversely in acquiring power over others. He thus has a very special and complex quality. We know full well how evil he is, but we have two sorts of sympathy for him in spite of that fact. One is our sympathy for the handicapped. The other is our natural sympathy for the chief character in a play who is trying to achieve a great end despite terrible odds. Though we condemn everything Richard does, we cannot help but admire the skill with which he does it. Richard must thus be extremely paradoxical in the effect he creates: repulsive and at the same time attractive; contemptible and at the same time mildly sympathetic; ridiculous and at the same time tragic; vulgar and at the same time glorious. As we meet Richard for the first time we must see all the evil in him. We must also see how it is possible for those who know him best to trust him implicitly and place their lives at his disposal. We must, finally, admire him and yet hate him with great passion.

THE SCENE

When he is addressing the audience directly, we may assume that a character is being completely honest. He is showing his deepest, most personal feelings about himself. All the disguise and hypocrisy which an evil person will normally assume when dealing with others will be dropped when he is completely alone, as Richard is now. Therefore, it is of the utmost importance that the actor sympathize with Richard in this scene and identify with the purposes Richard reveals. How is this possible? The actor must look into his own experience and recall some time when he has felt treated with great injustice and has desired revenge. It is that desire for revenge, which the average person feels but momentarily, that is the keynote of Richard's whole life. As a cripple he feels that the world has mistreated him, and that he must repay the world in full measure for its injustices.

As he begins this speech, which opens the play, Richard is caught in a paradox: the cause he has fought for, the triumph of the House of York, has been won. For everyone it should be a time of rejoicing; but Richard, because of his personal misery, cannot rejoice. This paradox does not become fully clear to the audience until "But I, that am not shaped for sportive tricks . . ." but it should be clear in Richard's mind at the outset, so that the feelings of triumph he reports have an undercurrent of gloom or cynicism in them. This effect can be achieved by a restraint of enthusiasm, a quiet calculatedness of speech that, while reflecting the triumph of the situation, does not wholeheartedly participate in it. It is important that the restraint should not become irritating or over-cynical, for Richard must make the audience like him during these first few lines. He must, in fact, seduce them into identifying their desires with his own in spite of themselves.

With metaphors of the season and the weather, Richard begins his picture of victory. The "winter of our discontent" was the time during which the members of the House of York fought to achieve power. The effect of the "glorious summer" is increased by our knowledge that the sun is taken as a symbol for the King. Thus Richard feels Edward of York to be a true king, shining brightly on the countryside, while there was, during the reign of Henry of Lancaster, a dimmer, more wintry sun.

The "clouds" represent the House of Lancaster, which stood between York and the sun of its own kingship. The water in these clouds has returned to its proper place in the ocean; that is to say, there is no further threat from the rival house. The scene is now not simply one of victory, but also of peace and gaiety. The weapons bruised in war can be hung up and treasured for the memories they recall. The sound of trumpets no longer is the signal for the army to charge into battle, but has become the music of a social gathering. The soldiers, accustomed to marching, now delight themselves with dancing. The god of war no longer frowns upon the countryside; the wrinkles are erased from his brow, and he joins in the fun, providing entertainment for a lady as her lover recounts for her at bedtime, perhaps, his deeds of valor in battle, while a lute accompanies his narrative.

Now Richard turns his attention away from the general scene of rejoicing to his own misery. Because he is a cripple, he cannot join with others in dancing and sporting events. Nor can he enjoy standing before a looking glass making himself handsome in order to attract some lady, preening himself as if to court the looking glass itself. The shape he has been given by nature is a rude, ugly one. He is incapable of strutting majestically before a glamorous and seductive young woman. Nature has cheated him out of the physical attractiveness that would make such pleasures possible for him. Born prematurely, he never developed properly; and his ugliness is so great that dogs bark at him, perhaps mistaking him for a beggar rather than a duke. It is important to observe at this point that Richard undoubtedly exaggerates the effect of his own deformity on others. Elsewhere in the play we see that he is seldom treated as one who is repulsive. Indeed, very shortly after this speech he puts his powers of seduction to the extreme test by wooing the Lady Anne (whose husband and father-in-law he has killed in battle) at the very moment when that lady is accompanying her dead father-in-law, King Henry VI, to his grave. Despite her initial horror, Lady Anne cannot resist Richard's advances and agrees to become his wife. There must certainly be something unusually attractive about Richard, or he could never win such a victory; and it is only his own exaggerated sense of what is probably a rather slight deformity that makes him believe he is as ugly as he says he is.

He dramatizes his plight by imagining that while others enjoy the relaxed, melodious delights of peace, there is nothing for him to do but observe his shadow in the sun and comment on his deformity. Because he cannot entertain others during these days when fine speaking is so widely enjoyed, Richard determines to express his hatred. The line, "I am determined to prove a villain" is one of the most difficult in the speech. It must be thought of as the logical consequence of the situation rather than as something that Richard expects to enjoy. If the actor can make the audience believe that the course of action he has chosen is, in his own terms, entirely reasonable and just, he will have achieved a great deal. In any event, he must not become melodramatic here, or the audience will become disgusted and lose much of its interest in the action that follows.

Richard now explains his plan to have Clarence, his brother, put to death by order of King Edward as a result of Edward's fear (instilled in him by Richard) that Clarence will murder his sons. The prophecy of which Richard has spoken to Edward is ambiguous. The "G" could stand for "George, Duke of Clarence." We know, however, that it stands for Gloucester, Richard's title. Richard's cleverness and rationality are further emphasized by his very accurate evaluation of Edward as "true and just," and of himself as "subtle, false and treacherous." It is a common Shakespearean irony for the true and just person to be used by the treacherous one to commit terrible crimes against the person he loves best, because he is too trusting to see the subtlety and deceit of the man who misleads him. This is Edward's present plight, for at Richard's suggestion he has had Clarence arrested. As the speech ends, Richard turns to see Clarence being led to the Tower. Immediately he changes his character. He is no longer the exposed villain we have been seeing, but suddenly becomes the loving and sympathetic younger brother who will promise to do everything in his power to help Clarence regain his favor with the King.

RICHARD ALONE

(Richard stands in the center of the stage. His left arm is crippled, and he can use it but little. He compensates for this by gesturing with his right arm both gracefully and flamboyantly. At first, however, he does not move. He simply stares at the audience as if hypnotizing them in order to get them to share his mood. Finally, on the word "buried" he points one finger of his right hand toward the ground in a peremptory manner, as if to say, "That gets rid of them.")

> Now is the winter of our discontent
> Made glorious summer by this sun of York;
> And all the clouds that lowered upon our house
> In the deep bosom of the ocean buried.

(He starts walking rather rapidly toward DR, limping just a little. His right hand circles his head on "wreaths," reaches into the air on "hung up.")

> Now are our brows bound with victorious wreaths,
> Our bruiséd arms hung up for monuments,

(He comes to a halt, and does a slight sarcastic bow on "meetings.")

> Our stern alarums changed to merry meetings,

(He extends his arm and points his toe, suggesting the beginning of a dance, again sarcastically.)

> Our dreadful marches to delightful measures.[1]

(He walks DLC slowly, deep in thought. Suddenly he stops and confronts the audience almost accusingly.)

> Grim-visaged war hath smoothed his wrinkled front,
> And now, instead of mounting barbéd [2] steeds

(His voice takes on a tone of very restrained mock melodrama.)

> To fright the souls of fearful adversaries,

(His voice drips sarcasm, mocking the lightness and joy of the scene of which he speaks so closely that it almost seems as if he is sharing it.)

> He capers nimbly in a lady's chamber
> To the lascivious[3] pleasing of a lute.

(From this point until line "And therefore, since I cannot prove a lover", Richard will move in a half circle from DLC to DR. He will do this in such manner that he seems to be wandering, almost groping his way about the back of the stage, much of the time having his back to the audience, but facing it each time he mentions an action that he cannot perform and mockingly pantomiming that action. The effect of this is partly to show the groping condition of Richard's spirit, and partly to dramatize his anger at the world. He should seem

48 / **Scenes to Perform**

Carl Becker as Richard III:
"Now are our brows bound with victorious wreaths,
Our bruiséd arms hung up for monuments."

to be walking away from the audience in contempt, turning now and then to hurl some vicious mockery at it. He is making the audience part of the world against which he wishes to vent his anger.)

> But I, that am not shaped for sportive tricks
> Nor made to court an amorous looking glass;
> I, that am rudely stamped, and want love's majesty
> To strut before a wanton ambling nymph;[4]
> I, that am cúrtailed of this fair proportion,
> Cheated of feature by dissembling[5] Nature,
> Deformed, unfinished, sent before my time
> Into this breathing world, scarce half made up,
> And that so lamely and unfashionable
> That dogs bark at me as I halt by them—
> Why, I, in this weak piping time of peace,
> Have no delight to pass away the time,
> Unless to see my shadow in the sun
> And descant[6] on mine own deformity.

(His tone changes to one of friendly objectivity. He is past anger now; he has become completely calculating. His right hand fingers the buttons on his coat. On the word "hate" he places his hand over his heart. The word is set apart from the rest of the sentence, but it is given no emotional coloring at all. Richard thus draws attention to the logical, rather than emotional character of his position.)

> And therefore, since I cannot prove a lover
> To entertain these fair well-spoken days,
> I am determinéd to prove a villain
> And hate the idle pleasures of these days.

(His tone continues to be friendly and objective. He smiles and nods at the audience, taking them into his confidence. His right hand plays nervously over his left hand and about the corners of his mouth.)

> Plots have I laid, inductions[7] dangerous,
> By drunken prophecies, libels, and dreams,
> To set my brother Clarence and the King
> In deadly hate the one against the other;

(Smiles and nods. Ambles toward DC as if he had no more to say. Suddenly turns to the audience and speaks with an attitude of intense sincerity.)

> And if King Edward be as true and just

(Becomes more introspective. Seems to be thinking about himself as if the audience were not present. Underplays this description of himself so that the entire effect is carried by the words themselves.)

> As I am subtle, false and treacherous,

(Seems to become aware once again that an audience is present. Intensifies his enthusiasm for what he is saying.)

This day should Clarence closely be mewed up[8]
About a prophecy

(*Looks quickly to both sides, as if to check that no one is listening. Then leans forward and points at the audience, as if taking them into his confidence.*)

which says that G
Of Edward's heirs the murderer shall be.

(*The satisfaction suddenly disappears from his face. He stands for a moment, gnawing his lip, as if he were thinking of something else. We must get a hint from this action of how little satisfaction Richard will derive from his deeds of cruelty. Then he seems to hear Clarence coming from L, and appears to be putting all his present thoughts out of his mind. The index finger of his left hand is held near his stomach, and pointed down, as if directing the thoughts to leave his mind.*)

Dive, thoughts, down to my soul: here Clarence comes!

(*He turns L, and his face acquires the radiant innocence that will make Clarence trust him.*)

NOTES

[1] *measures,* the slow and stately movements of a dance.
[2] *barbed,* having the breast and flanks armed.
[3] *lascivious,* tending to excite lustful desires.
[4] *wanton ambling nymph,* a young and beautiful woman strolling lustfully about.
[5] *dissembling,* false and hypocritical.
[6] *descant,* originally meaning, "to sing or warble," it came to mean, "to comment on."
[7] *induction,* initial step in an undertaking.
[8] *mewed up,* imprisoned.

VOCAL AND PHYSICAL CHARACTERIZATION

Richard's voice must have that same combination of beauty and ugliness that we have observed in his character. His words must be articulated with the greatest clarity: must, indeed, be over-subtle, reflecting the over-subtlety of his mind. We must hear in his voice that endearing quality that makes people trust him implicitly. Beneath it we must hear the viciousness, the pent-up hatred that, for a while at least, only we will be permitted to see. The actor can achieve this effect by exaggerating the tension in his lips and those parts of his mouth that shape the words. This exaggerated tension characterizes a person who has great difficulty with his coordination, but at the same time must try to impress others with his elegance. Through long efforts of concentration he has achieved articulation that has precision at the expense of true warmth. Richard's speech is part of the façade he has built in his own defense. It is perhaps nasal or guttural as a result of his deformity, but Richard has made of whatever unattractive basic vocal quality he has the most attractive possible results.

In order to suggest the undercurrent of viciousness that comes to the surface only when Richard is alone or under extreme tension, the actor should build up inside himself a tremendous feeling of bitterness, keep it there all the time, but deliberately suppress it most of the time. The effort to suppress the bitterness should give the character a nervous quality in his speech and behavior that will suggest slight physical instability or uneasiness and increase the sympathy of the listener for the man whose deformity he pities.

Richard's physical condition must be very real and of constant concern to him. It must be felt much more strongly internally than it is evidenced externally. Because he is sensitive to the scorn of others, Richard has made supreme efforts to disguise his deformity as much as possible, and has succeeded in making it barely visible. Thus, although he seems relatively graceful to others, he must work constantly to achieve this effect. He is very conscious of what he considers his own lack of grace. He should have a slight limp, a slight hump in the back, perhaps some restriction in the use of his arms. When John Barrymore played the role he achieved much of the effect by turning one foot inward. Richard must superimpose upon his deformity a majesty and elegance that will make others respect, honor, love, almost be hypnotized by him. His rapid rise to power would be impossible without these things. The actor must be aware that he is creating two very different images: one for the audience, and another for himself. The tension between these two wildly different images is a major part of the source of Richard's personal magnetism.

TO BE OR NOT TO BE

(from *Hamlet* by William Shakespeare)

To be, or not to be, that is the question:
Whether 'tis nobler in the mind to suffer
The slings and arrows of outrageous fortune
Or to take arms against a sea of troubles,
And by opposing end them. To die—to sleep—
No more; and by a sleep to say we end
The heartache, and the thousand natural shocks
That flesh is heir to. 'Tis a consummation
Devoutly to be wished. To die—to sleep.
To sleep—perchance to dream: ay, there's the rub!
For in that sleep of death what dreams may come
When we have shuffled off this mortal coil,
Must give us pause. There's the respect
That makes calamity of so long life.
For who would bear the whips and scorns of time,
The oppressor's wrong, the proud man's contumely,
The pangs of despiséd love, the law's delay,
The insolence of office, and the spurns
That patient merit of the unworthy takes,
When he himself might his quietus make
With a bare bodkin? Who would these fardels bear,
To grunt and sweat under a weary life,
But that the dread of something after death—
The undiscovered country, from whose bourn
No traveller returns—puzzles the will,
And makes us rather bear those ills we have
Than fly to others that we know not of?
Thus conscience does make cowards of us all,
And thus the native hue of resolution
Is sicklied o'er with the pale cast of thought,
And enterprises of great pith and moment
With this regard their currents turn awry
And lose the name of action.

COMMENTARY

THE PLAY

Hamlet is probably the source of more disagreement among critics, actors, directors, and audiences than any other play ever written. At the same time, every great actor longs to perform his interpretation of the melancholy Dane. No two productions of the play are likely to be very similar, nor are any two interpretations of a particular speech. Listen to recordings of Sir Laurence Olivier, Sir John Gielgud, Richard Burton, and Paul Scofield performing this soliloquy, and you will hear four very different interpretations. It is therefore particularly important to observe that the interpretation you find here is only one of many possibilities. As your understanding and love of the play grow you will want to work out your own interpretation, based on your personal weighing of the various elements in Hamlet's character and what you consider to be the proper balance between them. To do this well you will need an intimate knowledge of the entire play and familiarity with many different critical interpretations of it.

The scene is set in Denmark during the Middle Ages, but Shakespeare's thinking about what happens is nearly always in terms of his own country and his own time. Claudius, King of Denmark, has recently ascended the throne following the death of his brother, Hamlet. He has also married his brother's widow. Prince Hamlet, her son, mourns the death of his father and his mother's hasty remarriage. Upon learning from the ghost of his father that Claudius killed the elder Hamlet, the Prince vows revenge. In order to prevent Claudius from realizing that he seeks revenge, Prince Hamlet pretends to be mad. His delay in achieving his purpose, together with his previous feelings of depression, causes the Prince to contemplate suicide. In this scene he considers death and rejects it as a solution to his problems.

THE CHARACTER

Hamlet has been called a man who "could not make up his mind," a man "born ahead of his time," and a man of thought rather than action. None of these epithets captures the essence of his character, for it is one of contradictions. On the one hand he delays, perhaps excessively, in killing Claudius. On the other hand he takes sudden and decisive action many times during the play. On the one hand he is extremely sensitive to his mother's apparent lack of love for his dead father; on the other hand, he kills an important official in the court, one against whom he bears no excessive malice, and doesn't give the matter a second thought. Almost every action he takes is countered by some other action which contradicts it. Whatever the reason, Hamlet is primarily a man of contradictions, a man who cannot commit himself to any particular point of view or course of action; a skeptic. Under duress, Hamlet will decide on a course of action. When the compelling reasons for taking the action are no longer immediately felt he will lose interest in taking the action he has felt so important. This would present no problem were it not that Hamlet lays the greatest emphasis on consistency in others. He does not see how his mother could have loved his father and yet later love someone else. He does not see the possibility for Claudius to be anything but a villain, for his close friend Horatio to be anything but the ideal man, for a woman to be anything but frail, and so on. While his situation demands that he be highly adaptable to changing circumstances, his ideals condemn such adaptability. It is easy to see that Hamlet must become confused by his plight and simply wish to escape from it.

THE SCENE

In a soliloquy a character addresses the audience directly and tells them what he is thinking. Sometimes the soliloquy seems to be a direct glimpse into the character's mind; that is, to contain thoughts he would never speak to any other character. In this particular soliloquy Hamlet thinks, without particular reference to any events in the play, about the problem of suicide.

The question of suicide is of almost universal significance. Not only do most of us at some time in our lives seriously wish to die, but also we frequently debate the moral and philosophical questions of suicide, and of what consequences it might have for ourselves were we to take the decisive step. Perhaps this is one of the reasons why Hamlet's soliloquy is the single best known dramatic utterance ever written. It appeals to the world-weariness in all of us, and clearly and beautifully defines the fears that surround that condition.

"To be or not to be," says Hamlet, not "to live or to die." It is a question of existence as an individual human being, rather than a question of the biological continuation of life. The extreme simplicity of the two words gets to the core of everything important in life. It is total annihilation of personality that Hamlet postulates at the beginning of the speech, and it is this postulate that will soon prove unacceptable and defeat his purpose.

The question of nobility is raised, and the word answers its own question. Is it noble for a warrior to suffer an attack by a foe and not to fight back? Not in Shakespeare's world, where honor and nobility demand the ability to fight and insistence on fighting if one's honor has been impugned. Fortune is "outrageous," and one must almost certainly oppose it. Yet opposing fortune is an insane act: it is like marching with one's sword into the sea, attacking it as one goes. Yet miraculously the insanity of the act achieves victory. By opposing the sea of troubles, one ends not oneself but the troubles. The imagery is deliberately confusing here: it reflects the contradictions in Hamlet's mind, particularly the contradiction that by accepting death, which is the ultimate defeat, one can somehow achieve a victory.

"To die," says Hamlet, is nothing more than to sleep. And that sleep would end the thousand miseries that one inherits by being born. What more desirable end could one wish for? Again we find a contradiction, for Hamlet now speaks of the sin of suicide as something to be wished "devoutly." Has he, in rejecting the theological law against self-destruction, adopted a kind of religion in reverse?

Now we see a behavior pattern that is very typical of Hamlet. He has just arrived at an acceptable course of action when he draws back and reconsiders his reasoning. Like the true skeptic, he can always find a flaw in any logical process. The catch is that the sleep of death may bring dreams. What is the nature of these dreams? No one can say, for no traveler returns from death to tell us what the experience is like. It is possible, however, that the dreams are far more horrible than anything that could be experienced in life. One must therefore take pause before shedding the miseries of life. It is this "respect" for the possible terrors that may follow death that makes one live out one's life, even though the entire life may be a calamity.

Hamlet now lists the various sources of misery in life. The passage of time inevitably brings physical and mental anguish. One receives injustice from those in power, scorn from those who are proud, disappointment in love, delay in achieving one's legal rights, insolence from those holding official position, and rejection by the unworthy of those things that one has done patiently and meritoriously. Who would bear these things if he could achieve peace and quiet by putting a dagger in his breast? Who would bear these burdens but for the dread of something after death? It is this dread that confuses the determination to kill oneself and makes one accept miseries that are known rather than take a chance on the unknown. Thus the ability to think about the consequences of one's actions turns a man into a coward, and the natural color of resolution is made pale as a result of thinking about the consequences of the deed one has resolved to do. The most important actions that might be performed lose their direction as the result of thinking about consequences, and as a result are never fulfilled in action.

These are Hamlet's thoughts, but what is his mood? He is a man defeated by his own complexity and contradiction, a man struggling with an idea and finally exhausted by the struggle, a man who is humiliated by his inability to resolve life's greatest dilemmas. The hopefulness that Hamlet experiences at the beginning of the soliloquy when he believes that death may be a solution to his problems turns to bitterness and despair at the end, when he realizes that he must continue to accept life.

More particularly, his mood is communicated by the style of the language. Seldom does a thought have the length of the iambic pentameter line. Many of his units of thought are in groups of two or three words. Others are several lines long. Many lines are interrupted in the middle, and in the majority of cases the thought is continued without interruption from one line into the next. You can get a better idea of the effect of playing one rhythm against another if you compare Hamlet's speech with Tamburlaine's. Tamburlaine is a man of decisive and immediate action, not given to ruminating about the implications of an idea. Notice that his ideas tend to fall naturally into the rhythm of the iambic pentameter line, so that the thought closes with the line. Hamlet's failure to do this, his use of very irregular rhythms playing against the underlying iambic pentameter pattern, gives him a very nervous, contradictory, and indecisive quality.

Notice, too, the words that Hamlet selects. He condenses a great deal of meaning into a few words, so that a paraphrase of what he is saying must use many more words than he does. This shows that he has ruminated about these matters so often that his language has become very condensed, almost cryptic. His vocabulary is unusually rich, even for Shakespeare's day, as you will see again if you contrast his words with Tamburlaine's. Many of his words suggest action that is unusual in its connotations in relation to what he is describing (such as "shuffled off this mortal coil" for killing oneself—we would hardly think of suicide as a matter of "shuffling").

Finally, Hamlet uses speech that is very colloquial for his time, almost never stiff and formal. "Ay, there's the rub!" is one of many examples of this characteristic. The use of colloquial, casual constructions in the consideration of weighty matters is characteristic of Hamlet. It is related to the dark humor with which he often speaks about the matters that have tormented him most deeply. It is the casualness of despair, the giving up of those formalities that have so failed to make life rich and meaningful, the acknowledgement that there are no acceptable alternative formalities with which they can be replaced.

TO BE OR NOT TO BE

(Hamlet enters UL and crosses slowly to DR, his hands clasped at his waist. There he stands for a moment, looking out at the audience as if thinking. He should wait long enough to speak so that one suspects that he is not going to speak at all. In this way Hamlet will induce the audience to listen more closely

to what he has to say, and will also give himself a chance to consider the exact quality he wishes to give his words. When he finally does speak it is in an intense voice that rises only slightly above a whisper.)

  To be, or not to be, that is the question:

(He shifts his gaze slightly to the left.)

  Whether 'tis nobler in the mind to suffer
  The slings and arrows of outrageous fortune

(He shifts his gaze upwards and to the right.)

  Or to take arms against a sea of troubles,
  And by opposing

(He bows his head and closes his eyes, trying to experience the full, peaceful reality of death.)

    end them.

(He looks out at the audience, almost smiling, his voice having a tranquillity and near-happiness that conceals the seething misery that will shortly break to the surface.)

    To die—to sleep—
No more;

(His voice gathers enthusiasm. He feels that he is triumphing over the adversities of life.)

  and by a sleep to say we end
  The heartache, and the thousand natural shocks
  That flesh is heir to. 'Tis a consummation[1]
  Devoutly to be wished.

(He considers the previous statement again, this time less sure of his enthusiasm.)

    To die—to sleep.

(The statement becomes almost a question).

  To sleep—

(With terror, he sees a new possibility. The realization carries him a step or two backwards, and causes him to open his hands and deflect his gaze to the left.)

  perchance to dream:

(In terror, he reaches out and looks to the right, as if seeing some threatening reality in the distance.)

    ay, there's the rub!

(Draws into himself again, but this time there is uneasiness and despair in his voice, and perhaps bitterness too, resentment against the threatening reality he has just discovered.)

> For in that sleep of death what dreams may come
> When we have shuffled off this mortal coil,[2]

(*The tempo of his speech slows, as if he is forcing himself brutally to a halt, to a deeper awareness of what he must confront.*)

> Must give us pause.

(*He is rueful now. He shakes his head slightly, to show his reluctant acceptance of the continued pain of life.*)

> There's the respect
> That makes calamity of so long life.

(*He crosses DL, and addresses the audience more openly, appealing to them to share his reasoning.*)

> For who would bear the whips and scorns of time,
> The oppressor's wrong, the proud man's contumely,[3]
> The pangs of déspised love, the law's delay,
> The insolence of office,[4] and the spurns
> That patient merit of the unworthy takes,

(*He steps back, and his voice becomes somewhat more frenzied. The actor should resist the temptation to pantomime the action described in the lines.*)

> When he himself might his quietus[5] make
> With a bare bodkin[6]?

(*He crosses DC and addresses a different area of the audience, this time feeling the logic of his thought more intensely.*)

> Who would these fardels[7] bear,
> To grunt and sweat under a weary life,

(*Wonder creeps into his voice. It takes on something of an awed whisper.*)

> But that the dread of something after death—
> The undiscovered country, from whose bourn
> No traveller returns—puzzles the will,

(*His voice becomes heavier, more realistic.*)

> And makes us rather bear those ills we have

(*Gestures toward DL.*)

> Than fly to others that we know not of?

(*Crosses DR, heaves a deep sigh, and if a stool is available, sits on it.*)

> Thus conscience does make cowards of us all,

(*His voice gains greater firmness and decision.*)

> And thus the native hue of resolution
> Is sicklied o'er with the pale cast[8] of thought,

Lester Allen as Hamlet: "Thus conscience does make cowards of us all."

(*Rises, slowly, his fist clenched in front of him.*)

And enterprises of great pith and moment[9]
With this regard their currents turn awry[10]
And lose the name of action.

NOTES

[1] *consummation,* outcome.
[2] *coil,* turmoil.
[3] *contumely,* haughty and contemptuous rudeness.
[4] *office,* people holding official position.
[5] *quietus,* full discharge (a legal term).
[6] *bodkin,* dagger.
[7] *fardels,* burdens.
[8] *cast,* color.
[9] *moment,* importance.
[10] *awry,* with a twist to one side.

VOCAL AND PHYSICAL CHARACTERIZATION

The best clue to the way Hamlet sounds and acts is given us by his rejected lover, Ophelia, when she describes the way Hamlet was before he went mad. "The courtier's, soldier's, scholar's/Eye, tongue, sword." This means that when Hamlet was himself, he set the standard for all courtiers in the eloquence of his speech, for all scholars in the keenness of his eyes, for all soldiers in the deftness of his swordsmanship. While this is probably a biased opinion, it suggests that Hamlet was indeed a man capable of highly polished behavior and manners. The individual actor must decide how far Hamlet has fallen from the elegance he once had as a result of his deep depression, but he must always maintain traces of that elegance. No man can shed lifelong habits easily. To emphasize his grief, Hamlet dresses in black and speaks cryptically to those around him, but time and again he returns to his former elegance.

To the extent that he has not been immobilized by his grief, he speaks with a voice that is beautiful to listen to, and with diction which is refined and elegant without being in any sense unmasculine. In a speech to a group of traveling actors, Hamlet tells us something about how he moves:

> Do not saw the air too much with your hand, thus; but use all gently . . . Suit the action to the word, the word to the action, with this special observance, that you o'erstep not the modesty of nature; . . . O there be players that I have seen play and heard others praise, and that highly (not to speak it profanely), that, neither having th' accent of Christians nor the gait of Christian, pagan, nor man, have so strutted and bellowed that I have thought some of Nature's journeymen had made men, and not made them well, they imitated humanity so abominably.

It would seem logical to suppose that if in the midst of his grief Hamlet can still worry about the qualities he speaks of to the actors, he would maintain them in his own character, walking and speaking with grace, ease, and perfect posture. He must not be awkward, "sawing the air" with his hands, or strutting. He must not be over-graceful either, for later in the play he makes fun of this quality in one of the courtiers.

The opening portion of the soliloquy should be calm and restrained, as Hamlet considers the peace of being free from his miseries. On "perchance to dream" his mood suddenly changes. He recoils, but not melodramatically so, from the dreams. Now the tempo of his speech quickens and his voice becomes stronger as he faces in his imagination all those qualities of fortune he most despises. At the line "thus conscience does make cowards of us all," he slackens his pace with the depression that follows having faced an unpleasant reality. This depression grows and becomes ever deeper and harder as he moves toward the end of the soliloquy.

HARPAGON SEARCHES FOR HIS STOLEN MONEY

(from *The Miser* by Molière)

Thieves! Thieves! Murder! Stop the murderers! Justice! Just Heaven! I am lost! I am killed; they have cut my throat; they have stolen my money. Who can it be? What has become of him? Where is he? Where does he hide himself? What shall I do to find him? Where to run? Where not to run? Is he not there? Who is it? Stop! (*To himself, pressing his own arm.*) Give me back my money, scoundrel . . . Ah, it is myself! My senses are wandering, and I do not know where I am, who I am, and what I am doing. Alas! My poor money! my poor money! My dearest friend, they have deprived me of you; and as you are taken from me, I have lost my support, my consolation, my joy: everything is at an end for me, and I have nothing more to do in this world. Without you, life becomes impossible. It is all over; I am utterly exhausted; I am dying; I am dead; I am buried. Is there no one who will resuscitate me by giving me back my beloved money, or by telling me who has taken it? Eh! what do you say? There is no one. Whoever he is who has done this, he must have carefully watched his hour; and he has just chosen the time when I was speaking to my wretch of a son. Let us go. I must inform the authorities, and have the whole of my household examined; female-servants, male-servants, son, daughter, and myself also. What an assembly! I do not look at any one whom I do not suspect, and every one seems to be my thief. Eh! what are they speaking of yonder? Of him who has robbed me? What noise is that up there? Is it my thief who is there? For pity's sake, if you know any news of my thief, I implore you to tell me. Is he not hidden among you? They are all looking at me, and laughing in my face. It will turn out that they have, no doubt, a share in the robbery. Come quickly, magistrates, police-officers, provosts, judges, instruments of torture, gibbets, and executioners. I will have the whole world hanged; and if I do not recover my money, I will hang myself afterwards.

COMMENTARY

THE PLAY

It has been said of Molière that his genius lay in the fact that he raised comedy to the heights of tragedy. That is, he found in the purely farcical situations that dominated earlier comedies the possibility of bringing to life characters who reflected the absurdities of human nature that we recognize as universal. It was the nature of the characters, rather than mere coincidence or the author's contrivance, that brought about the situations on which his comedies depended. Yet his characters and situations were not limited by realism. Molière was capable of heightening them so that they became larger and more fascinating than real life without losing the universals on which they were based.

Harpagon is the prototype of the man who lives for his money. He has two children, each of whom wishes to marry, but both of whom are held in check by their father's greed. Indeed, the old man has determined that he himself will marry the girl his son is in love with. In desperation, Cléante, his son, tries to borrow money so that he can afford to elope with the girl. The money lender to whom he is led turns out to be his own father.

Harpagon has a pot of money buried in his garden, but he keeps digging it up and putting it in different places for fear it will be discovered and stolen. When it is indeed stolen, he is almost beside himself; and we are treated to one of the most famous and delightful scenes in all comedy, in which the miser tries to find the thief. It is Cléante who ultimately finds the money, but he refuses to return it to his father unless he is allowed to marry the girl he loves. Faced with the choice between his money and a beautiful wife, Harpagon quickly decides on the former, and both the happy couples are united.

The Character

Molière has created a man with a single passion that dominates his life who is, however, not a stereotype. The situations in which Harpagon is placed cause him in different ways to show the passion he has for money while he is trying to pursue other goals. We see the extent of this passion not only through its direct expression, but also through numerous opportunities to compare it with other, quite normal human motivations. There is an important difference between a comic character who thinks of one thing only, and one who thinks of many things, but whose thinking is constantly distorted by one domineering passion. The former type has little dimension; the latter, a great deal, and it is the latter that we have here. We see Harpagon in love; we see him as a parent; we see him as the master of a household; and in all these roles we see him as a man whose life is distorted by his passion for money. The actor must make us believe in a man who really does love money more deeply than he loves anything else.

The Scene

Harpagon has just ascertained that his money has, indeed, been stolen. He rushes onstage calling out for help, first to anyone who might be passing by, and then to heaven. Quickly his thoughts turn to his own condition. He is no longer crying for help; he is bemoaning the fate that has left him without the foundation on which his life is built. The pain is experienced as almost a physical thing. In the progression, "I am killed; they have cut my throat; they have stolen my money," each statement reflects a deeper pain than the previous one. Like a person who has hit his thumb with a hammer, Harpagon feels the pain gradually growing and accumulating.

Next, his thoughts turn to the culprit. Perhaps he can still be found before he gets away. It is the moment of hope that what is lost can still be recovered that comes before the loss can be fully accepted. He is searching for the thief, wondering in which direction to run. In the process of looking in different places he turns so rapidly that he seizes his own arm. Harpagon's excitement at having caught the villain is so great that it prevents his feeling the pressure of his grasp on his own arm. His perplexity that it is himself he has caught should not be anticipated; it should be a real discovery and a sorrowful one for him.

Indeed, the disappointment is so strong that for a moment Harpagon thinks he is out of his mind. He cannot face what has happened to him, and forgets where he is and who he is, being conscious only of a generalized grief and helplessness. Slowly the memory comes back to him. He weeps for his money as one might weep for a child who is lost. Suddenly he realizes the intensity of his feeling for that money. It is his dearest friend, closer to him than any human being ever could be. It is not what the money represents or what it will buy, but the actual coins themselves that he is missing, and he experiences the direct personal anguish of one who has lost a lover. The emptiness of a life that will henceforward be meaningless hovers over him. He becomes emotionally exhausted, collapsing on the ground like one dead.

Despair has exhausted him. A new, much cooler querulousness seizes him. Perhaps someone will take pity on his miserable condition and tell him who has taken the money. He cries out, hoping that someone will answer him, even thinking for a moment that he hears an answer; but there is no answer, and he is crushed.

Having been disappointed in his plea for pity, he becomes crafty. He tries to puzzle out the thinking of the man who has stolen his money. It must be someone in his own household who could wait for just the right opportunity. The thought that he was speaking to his son at the moment of the theft makes him angry at the boy. But he is satisfied that he has found a solution. He will go to the authorities and have everyone in his household examined, including himself. He throws up his hands, realizing how many possible culprits there are. Just as he thinks everyone who surrounds him would do anything to increase his supply of money, so, he knows, would he himself as well. Therefore it seems quite natural to him to include himself in the list of suspects. It is this touch that gives us a great deal of insight into the empty world in which Harpagon lives, for he can imagine no motive except the desire for money, and consequently cannot derive pleasure from any human relationship.

Now, as a result of his intense misery, Harpagon begins to hear the voices of people who are not there. He rushes to one corner of the stage, thinking he overhears a conversation about the robber. A sound on the other side of the stage distracts him, and he rushes to investigate that.

Suddenly a very unusual thing happens. He turns to the audience and addresses it directly, making it a part of the action of the play. The shock of this sudden shift of the audience's role from spectator to participant is very great, and there is no way to reduce it. The actor should realize this, and make the most of it. His remarks to the audience have until now been those accepted as conventional in a soliloquy: a revelation of what is passing through the character's mind. Harpagon is now making us laugh at the absurdity of that convention by reminding us that we have been there watching the whole time. We suddenly become conscious of ourselves as spectators, and we laugh self-consciously. Harpagon then picks up our laughter and uses it in the play. He is upset by it. It is proof to him that no one takes his problem seriously. He talks to the audience about what the audience is doing, and he thereby divides us into two selves: the spectators and the participants. This is one of the most unusual and brilliant parodies of dramatic convention to be found anywhere in the literature of the theatre. It is effective because the audience has been so deeply involved in the action and in the character of Harpagon that it has forgotten to be aware of itself as an audience. Harpagon's ability to remind us that he is only a character in a play and that we are spectators of that play by momentarily denying the truth of this makes us marvel at the extent to which Molière has made us believe in him as a character.

Harpagon decides that the audience is against him, is trying to conceal the thief, and he accuses it of having a share in the subterfuge. In his anger a flood of words associated with agencies of the law comes to mind. He shouts all these things in a desperate effort to get the help he needs. So deep is Harpagon's pain that he wishes to destroy the whole world. When he has done so, if he does not get his money back, he will not wish to live either.

What makes this scene so fascinating is that it is always threatening to turn into tragedy. Harpagon is a man who suffers so deeply over the loss of his money that he tempts us to take pity on him. But each time we are on the verge of doing so, he does something to increase the absurdity of the situation and thereby to still our pity. Such moments when one emotion threatens to become a totally different one are invariably moments of great theatrical excitement if they are handled so that they are believable. If the actor can rise to the occasion, he has here an opportunity for the finest dramatic achievement.

HARPAGON SEARCHES FOR HIS STOLEN MONEY

(*Harpagon rushes onstage from UL to C, shouting*)

Thieves! Thieves! Murder!

(*He stands C, hands outstretched to the audience.*)

Stop the murderers!

(*He runs DR, as if calling to someone standing just offstage.*)

Justice!

(*He raises his hands pleadingly to heaven, clasping them together. This he does quickly following the preceding action, so that one action flows into the other.*)

Just Heaven! I am lost!

(*He brings his clasped hands down slowly from above his head to the level of his chest, bowing his head in pain.*)

I am killed; they have cut my throat; they have stolen my money.

(*He looks around him suspiciously, as if hoping to see the criminal somewhere onstage.*)

Who can it be? What has become of him? Where is he?

(*If there is a piece of furniture onstage, he gets upstage of it and looks under it. If not, he simply feels around on the floor in front of him, or perhaps examines the curtain.*)

Where does he hide himself?

(*Gives it up, sits back on his heels, scratching his head or gesturing helplessly.*)

What shall I do to find him?

(*Starts to run DL, stops, gestures helplessly to the audience.*)

Where to run?

(*Points to all the exits in turn.*)

Where *not* to run?

(*Thinks he sees someone UR. Scurries up to the exit, stops and looks offstage.*)

Is he not there?

(*Thinks he sees someone else at the DR exit. Runs to it. This time the arm that is on the downstage side trails behind him.*)

Who is it?

(*Suddenly turns and seizes his own downstage arm by the wrist, thinking it belongs to someone else. He struggles with it with contained violence.*)

Stop! Give me back my money, scoundrel . . .

(*Realizes that it is his own arm he is holding. Lets it drop with a mixture of chagrin and disgust. Looks pathetically at the audience.*)

Ah, it is myself!

(*Staggers toward C, left hand pressed to forehead, palm out.*)

My senses are wandering, and I do not know where I am, who I am, and what I am doing.

(*Kneels C. Looks completely despondent.*)

Alas! My poor money!

(*Beats his fists on the floor, crying like a baby.*)

My poor money!

(*Clasps his hands in front of him, sobbing.*)

My dearest friend, they have deprived me of you; and as you are taken from me, I have lost my support, my consolation, my joy:

(*He speaks more rapidly, almost choking on his sobs.*)

everything is at an end for me, and I have nothing more to do in this world.

(*Stands, raises his hands high in the air, looking intensely dramatic. He declaims this in a loud oratorical voice.*)

Without you, life becomes impossible.

68 / Scenes to Perform

(With each phrase he lowers himself part way to the floor, so that on the phrase "I am buried" he can fall sprawled out flat on his face.)

It is all over; I am utterly exhausted; I am dying; I am dead; I am buried.

(Despair has given him a kind of coolness. He raises his head, supports his chin with his elbow and speaks in a very dry voice with an almost offhand quality.)

Is there no one who will resuscitate me by giving me back my beloved money, or by telling me who has taken it?

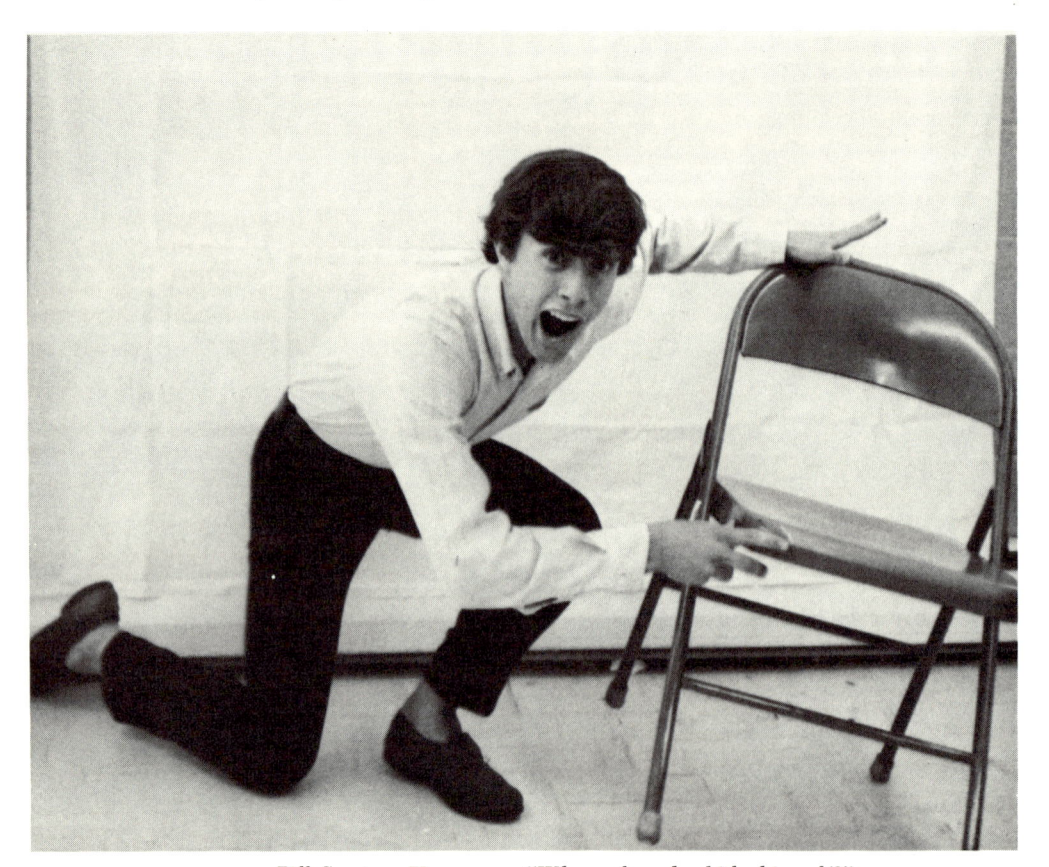

Bill Swet as Harpagon: "Where does he hide himself?"

(Thinks he hears something. Springs to his feet, cupping his hand to his ear, L.)

Eh! what do you say?

(Listens for a moment, then drops his hand in despair.)

There is no one.

(Comes forward and addresses the audience confidentially. He is thinking very carefully now, trying to reason out the motives of the culprit.)

Whoever he is who has done this, he must have carefully watched his hour; and he has just chosen the time when I was speaking to my wretch of a son.

(*He nods, having found the solution, pointing a finger at the audience, affirming that solution.*)

Let us go.

(*He starts walking L in a very businesslike way, feeling certain now he knows exactly what to do.*)

I must inform the authorities, and have the whole of my household examined; female-servants, male-servants, son, daughter, and myself also.

(*Throws up his hands in despair, realizing how many possible culprits there are.*)

What an assembly! I do not look at anyone whom I do not suspect, and everyone seems to be my thief.

(*Suddenly hears someone talking offstage R. Runs over to the DR exit, and cups his hand, listening.*)

Eh! What are they speaking of yonder? Of him who has robbed me?

(*Before he can answer his own question, he responds to an offstage noise UL, and rushes to that exit, speaking as he goes, and then peering offstage.*)

What noise is that up there? Is it my thief who is there?

(*Gives it up, comes DC, addresses audience directly.*)

For pity's sake, if you know any news of my thief, I implore you to tell me. Is he not hidden among you?

(*Steps back, horrified.*)

They are all looking at me, and laughing in my face.

(*Nods his head knowingly, almost vindictively.*)

It will turn out that they have, no doubt, a share in the robbery.

(*Suddenly flies into a violent rage, and rushes about the stage shouting out through different exits as he comes to them.*)

Come quickly, magistrates, police-officers, provosts, judges, instruments of torture, gibbets, and executioners.

(*Stands in the exact center of the stage trying to look as much as possible like an avenging demon.*)

I will have the whole world hanged;

(Moves slowly DC, red in the face from holding back tears and violent rage, hands almost clawing the air, telling the audience all, not because he trusts them, but because he can no longer contain himself.)

and if I do not recover my money, I will hang myself afterwards.

VOCAL AND PHYSICAL CHARACTERIZATION

Years of seclusion and gloating over his moneybags have made Harpagon seem older than he is and have given him a deformed appearance. The shoulders are hunched, the neck thrust forward, the arms and legs stiff at the joints. He moves with a somewhat jerky, clumsy motion and has a tendency to get tangled up in his own body when he tries to move too rapidly. His eyes are wide open, as it is difficult for him to see any distance; and he is desperately trying to keep an eye on his money. The confusion about what is going on around him and the inability to relate separate events easily are characteristic of very nearsighted people whose vision has not been corrected. He has a haunted, almost persecuted appearance. His chin is thrust forward, giving him a determined expression.

Harpagon is short of breath from age and lack of exercise. Therefore he speaks in short, choppy phrases that have a clipped, defiant, even paranoid sound. In this scene he gets out of breath quickly, and is therefore breathing very heavily. His voice is dry and rasping, having the edginess and rigidity that come with age, and that can be reproduced by using a nasal voice, short phrases, and occasional repetition. If the physical characterization is right, it will help with the sound of the voice. Hume Cronyn, when he portrayed this role, used the image of the sidewise-moving crab. The stiffness and abruptness of this kind of motion will almost naturally be echoed in the voice. This impression is further reinforced by the name Molière has chosen, for Harpagon means grappling hook.

Though the voice is dry and thin-sounding, there must be enough support so that it does not get too much out of control on the loud passages in which Harpagon is bemoaning his fate. Keep a solid column of air underneath it at all times, not to give it a husky sound, but rather to act as a buffer against the punishment the voice will have to take when Harpagon hysterically wails about the loss of his money. Remember, too, that Harpagon's particular kind of misery makes him very agile in this scene, and that his voice must be capable of reflecting a great variety of attitudes and feelings.

LORD FOPPINGTON'S DAY

(from *The Relapse* by Sir John Vanbrugh)

The inside of a book, I must confess, I am nat altogether so fand of. Far to mind the inside of a book, is to entertain one's self with the forced product of another man's brain. Naw I think a man of quality and breeding may be much better diverted with the natural sprouts of his own. But to say the truth, madam, let a man love reading never so well, when once he comes to know this tawn, he finds so many better ways of passing the four-and-twenty hours, that 'twere ten thousand pities he should consume his time in that. Far example, madam, my life; my life, madam, is a perpetual stream of pleasure, that glides through such a variety of entertainments, I believe the wisest of our ancestors never had the least conception of any of 'em. I rise, madam, about ten a-clack. I don't rise sooner, because 'tis the worst thing in the world for the complexion; nat that I pretend to be a beau; but a man must endeavor to look wholesome, lest he make so nauseous a figure in the side-bax, the ladies should be compelled to turn their eyes upon the play. So, at ten a-clack, I say, I rise. Naw, if I find 'tis a good day, I resalve to take a turn in the Park, and see the fine women; so huddle on my clothes, and get dressed by one. If it be nasty weather, I take a turn in the chocolate-house: where, as you walk, madam, you have the prettiest prospect in the world; you have looking-glasses all raund you. From thence I go to dinner at Lacket's, where you are so nicely and delicately served, that, stap my vitals! they shall compose you a dish no bigger than a saucer, shall come to fifty shillings. Between eating my dinner (and washing my mouth, ladies) I spend my time, till I go to the play; where, till nine a-clack, I entertain myself with looking upon the company; and usually dispose of one hour more in leading 'em aut. So there's twelve of the four-and-twenty pretty well over. The other twelve, madam, are disposed of in two articles: in the first four I toast myself drunk, and in t'other eight I sleep myself sober again. Thus, ladies, you see my life is an eternal raund "O" of delights.

COMMENTARY

THE PLAY

Colley Cibber* began his acting career at the Drury Lane Theater, London, in 1690, as an apprentice without pay. Despite a number of lucky chances, he remained in virtual obscurity for the next six years and was considered a very poor actor. Finally

* Pronounced "Sibber".

in 1696 he wrote a comedy called *Love's Last Shift,* which had a part in it for himself. Though the comedy was very fine indeed, the management was dubious about taking a chance on Cibber's acting. It did, however, and, as Sir Novelty Fashion he performed extremely well, so well, in fact, that Sir John Vanbrugh was inspired to write a sequel to Cibber's play, entitled *The Relapse.* In it Sir Novelty appeared again, this time having been promoted to the peerage and given the title Lord Foppington. The new play made Cibber's reputation, for he was an immediate success as Foppington, and appeared in the role repeatedly throughout his entire life. To make a good thing even better, Cibber wrote a second sequel, *The Careless Husband,* in which the same character appeared once more.

Love's Last Shift followed the adventures of one Loveless, who attempted to be unfaithful to his wife, Amanda, only to meet her disguised as his mistress and pledge his speedy reform. The play has been called the first sentimental comedy, for it differed from other plays of the time in that it did not commit itself to an immoral point of view. *The Relapse* derives its name from the fact that in it Loveless has a relapse and becomes infatuated with a pretty cousin of Amanda's. Various attempts are made to arouse Amanda's jealousy and make her be unfaithful to her husband, but she remains a woman of high virtue and is mainly responsible for the play's moral tone.

Lord Foppington makes a single rather clumsy attempt to seduce Amanda and gets himself stabbed in the attempt. He is chiefly involved in a subplot, however, in which he has purchased the right to marry a simple country girl named Hoyden, whose father is a very rich man. He is tricked by his brother, Tom, who disguises himself as Lord Foppington and marries Hoyden first. Lord Foppington's reaction to this is interesting. He says:

Now for my part, I think the wisest thing a man can do with an aching heart is to put on a serene countenance; for a philosophical air is the most becoming thing in the world to the face of a person of quality. I will therefore bear my disgrace like a great man, and let people see I am above an affront.

To which Tom replies:

Your lordship may keep up your spirits with your grimace if you please; I shall support mine with this lady, and two thousand pounds a year.

THE CHARACTER

There can be little doubt that Cibber made such a hit as Lord Foppington because he had a great deal in common with the character he played. He was a man of undaunted optimism as to his own prospects, one who reacted to all his setbacks much as we have seen that Lord Foppington does. He was, in addition, such a snob that he alienated almost everyone who knew him. He was very fond of dressing well, and one of his touches as Lord Foppington was to enter bare-headed and have an enormous wig brought on stage in a sedan chair and placed ceremoniously upon his head.

As a husband and father he proved himself far more devoted to the gambling table than to the family hearth, and he once remarked upon losing his week's salary at cards, "Now I must go home and eat a child!" We have an overall impression of a man who was exclusively interested in himself.

Lord Foppington is a man for whom people have only the most superficial reality. His life is a continual pose, designed to impress others, and he is never aware that he arouses only their mirth. Because he has no inner reality, he puts all of his qualities on the surface—and a magnificent surface it is, with its elegant gestures, its peacock-like strut, its elaborately overdressed high fashion, its plumed three-cornered hat, and its continual use of the snuffbox and the handkerchief. The best guide to the character of Lord Foppington is the portrait of Cibber in the part.

Lord Foppington arouses our laughter because he is so absurd. The epilogue to *The Relapse* hastens to assure us that he is also harmless:

> All treasons come from slovens, it is nat
> Within the reach of gentle beaux to plat;
> They have no gall, no spleen, no teeth,
>   no stings,
> Of all Gad's creatures, the most harmless
>   things.
> Through all record, no prince was ever slain
> By one who had a feather in his brain.
> They're men of too refined an education,
> To squabble with a court—for a vile dirty
>   nation.

* * * * * *

> Did every highwayman yet bid you stand,
> With a sweet bawdy snuff-box in his hand?

And concludes by saying that the play's author is a dog for having so slandered such gentle and lawful creatures as the beaux by laughing at them.

The Scene

Lord Foppington has engaged Amanda in conversation with the idea of so impressing her with himself that he will find it easy to seduce her later. The conversation has turned to books, and we find that Lord Foppington, like many nonconformists, retains his individualism primarily through ignorance. He does not allow his mind to become contaminated by perusing the inside of a book and thus bringing it into contact with other men's ideas. Rather than read for his education, Lord Foppington contents himself with developing his own narrow-minded approach to things and parading it as original wisdom.

As a conventional, insincere excuse for having been so egotistical, Lord Foppington paints a picture of London as a place where a man is kept so busy that he has no time for reading. He gloats over the advantages one of his own time has over "the wisest of our ancestors." He has only the most superficial notion of what these advantages are: they seem to reduce to parading one's charms in front of the ladies.

Reversing the notion that rising early in the morning is a means to good health, Lord Foppington lies in bed until ten for the benefit of his complexion. With a touch of false modesty he denies that he pretends to be a beau (the one thing he unquestionably is). Rather, he claims that it is out of a sense of public duty that he takes care of his complexion. When he attends the theatre and conspicuously locates himself in a box seat, if he is attractive, he will provide the ladies with a beautiful sight; but if he is unattractive they will be compelled to watch the play.

This remark, coming from a character in a play, is a very revealing one. Actors and playwrights at the time were much concerned that the audience typically had the annoying habit of paying attention to the play only when it was entertaining. If the audience did not care for an actor's performance, it would hiss him off the stage. If it did not like the play, it would become restless during the performance and engage in loud conversation until it was no longer possible to follow what was going on.

Cibber, the actor, was so fond of plays that he would go to see them whenever he was not performing in them. Yet the remark is typical of something he himself might have said—a remark full of laughter at himself but satirizing also the attitudes of those who disagreed with him. The point is that while Lord Foppington is superficial, he is not incapable of occasionally poking fun at his own absurdity. The actor who does not capture this quality will reduce the character to a stereotype and make him far less interesting than he actually is.

Lord Foppington, planning to spend the early part of the day either in the Park or the chocolate house, depending on the weather, spends three hours in dressing, or, as he puts it, "huddling on his clothes." The word "huddle," which suggests that Lord Foppington gathered his clothes about him in a clumsy and hurried way, belies the care with which he actually put them on, making sure that every ribbon and piece of lace was in exactly the right order. Here is a combination of exaggeration and understatement that can be very funny if the actor neither misses it nor underplays it.

If he goes to the Park, Lord Foppington will enjoy watching the fine women. If he goes to the chocolate house, he will have an even more delightful time watching himself in the mirrors as he parades up and down. In Lord Foppington's day the Park and the chocolate house were, like the playhouses, very fashionable places to appear if you were a member of the rising middle class and were trying to make yourself appear somewhat more important than you actually were.

Next Lord Foppington shows his predilection for conspicuous consumption. At Locket's the dinner you are served is very small and very expensive. That is taken as evidence that it must be very fine indeed.

The phrase "stap my vitals," which Lord Foppington is fond of and uses throughout the play, means something like, "You wouldn't believe it, but you may cut my throat if what I say isn't absolutely true." It shows the speaker's love of the dramatic, his feigned incredulity at what he has observed, and his sense of his own superiority for being above wanting to believe such a thing. It is another aspect of Lord Foppington's tendency to excess in all things, and should be read with an air of habitual and dramatic elegance.

Having eaten his dinner, Lord Foppington goes to the play, which begins at six. There he entertains himself by watching the audience. Performances in his time continued until after ten. After a long, full-length play there would be an after-piece, which was usually a farce with music. Thus, Lord Foppington habitually leaves before the performance is over, perhaps before the feature presentation is over. In leaving, he makes a great disturbance and takes a large part of the audience with him. He would have us believe that it takes him an hour to make his exit from the playhouse.

He spends the rest of the evening getting drunk, and then goes home to sleep off the effects.

This portrait of the fop, in which Vanbrugh gives dimensionality to a character most likely to be denied it, is a beautifully done satirical picture of one segment of life in the 18th century.

LORD FOPPINGTON'S DAY

(*Lord Foppington stands center, facing slightly to the right. Amanda and her cousin Berinthia stand listening DR. Loveless stands just to the left of Foppington. Before he speaks, Foppington takes a pinch of snuff from the snuffbox he holds in his left hand and sneezes.*)

The inside of a book, I must confess,

(*Gestures with the palm of his right hand, as if rejecting the book.*)

I am nat altogether so fand of.

(*Smiles, leans forward slightly, gestures with his right hand palm up.*)

Far to mind the inside of a book, is to entertain one's self with the forced product of another man's brain.

(*Stands bolt upright, places the finger tips of his right hand on his chest, keeping his right elbow as high as the wrist. Places his left hand on his left hip.*)

Naw I think a man of quality and breeding may be much better diverted

(*Circles his right hand above his head, suggesting a "sprout" from his brain.*)

with the natural sprouts of his own.

(*Takes another pinch of snuff and sneezes. Tilts his head modestly to the left, casting a glance at Loveless and then looking back at the ladies.*)

But to say the truth, madam, let a man love reading never so well,

(*Gestures with his right hand, palm up, partially cupped, index finger pointing.*)

when once he comes to know this tawn,

(*Finger tips of his right hand to his chest.*)

he finds so many better ways of passing the four-and-twenty hours,

(*Both arms open out slowly, palms of hands up.*)

that 'twere ten thousand pities he should consume his time in that.

(*Takes a step toward Amanda, pointing the index finger of his right hand at her.*)

Far example, madam,

(*Pulls from his left cuff a handkerchief, which he spins rapidly in wide circles with his extended right hand as he bows deeply.*)

my life;

(*Touches the handkerchief to his lips as he straightens up, then replaces it in the cuff.*)

my life, madam, is a perpetual

(*Draws a straight line very daintily in the air about one foot long directly in front of him with his right hand. Rolls the "r" in "stream."*)

stream of pleasure,

(*Pulls out the handkerchief again; twirls it in the air as he assumes a number of different poses in quick succession.*)

(Portrait in the Garrick Club, painted by G. Grisoni, engraved by J. Simon.)

Colley Cibber as Lord Foppington: "As you walk, Madam, you have the prettiest prospect in the world; you have looking glasses all raund you."

that glides through such a variety of entertainments, I believe the wisest of our ancestors never had the least conception of any of 'em.

(*Crosses, DL, stuffing the handkerchief back in his cuff.*)

I rise, madam, about ten a-clack.

(*Having shifted the snuffbox to the right hand, he turns, pointing the left hand at the ladies, so that he is now facing them across the stage.*)

I don't rise sooner, because 'tis the worst thing in the world for the complexion;

(*Transfers the snuffbox again to the left hand, again pulls out the handkerchief, and bows as before, smiling broadly.*)

nat that I pretend to be a beau;

(*Speaks the next very rapidly, while stuffing the handkerchief back in his cuff.*)

but a man must endeavor to look wholesome, lest he make so nauseous a figure in the side-bax, the ladies should be compelled to turn their eyes upon the play.

(*Adjusts his coat at the bottom by pulling it down a little on the word "rise."*)

So, at ten a-clack, I say, I rise.

(*Crosses slowly, majestically toward the ladies, DR.*)

Naw, if I find 'tis a good day, I resalve to take a turn in the Park, and see the

(*Winks at them, laughs.*)

fine women;

(*Speaks quickly and briskly, as if to deny the implications of what he has just done. Suggests the motions of adjusting his clothing.*)

so huddle on my clothes, and get dressed by one.

(*Cross C.*)

If it be nasty weather, I take a turn in the chocolate-house:

(*Turns, facing the ladies.*)

where, as you walk, madam, you have the prettiest prospect in the world;

(*Poses, as if admiring himself in the looking-glasses.*)

you have looking-glasses all raund you.

(*Cross DL.*)

From thence I go to dinner at Lacket's, where you are so nicely and delicately served, that,

(*Turns, facing them, and looking expectant about what, in the imagination, he is about to be served.*)

    stap my vitals! they shall compose you a dish no bigger than

(*Holds his hands in the shape of a saucer placed before him.*)

    a saucer, shall come to

(*Index finger of right hand up.*)

    fifty shillings.

(*Takes snuff, pulls out the handkerchief, applies it to his nose, then gestures with the right hand out, holding the handkerchief.*)

    Between eating my dinner

(*Applies the handkerchief daintily to his lips.*)

    (and washing my mouth, ladies)

(*Right hand, holding handkerchief, down to waist level.*)

    I spend my time, till I go to the play; where, till nine a-clack, I entertain myself with looking upon the company; and usually dispose of one more hour in

(*Cross C.*)

    leading 'em aut.

(*Faces the ladies, stuffs the handkerchief back in his cuff.*)

    So there's twelve of the four-and-twenty pretty well over.

(*Both arms out.*)

    The other twelve, madam, are disposed of in two articles: in the first four

(*Right hand raised in a gesture of toasting.*)

    I toast myself drunk, and in t'other eight

(*Right hand raised, palm out, to eye, suggesting slumber.*)

    I sleep myself sober again.

(*Faces them, smiles.*)

    Thus, ladies, you see my life

(*Quickly pulls out the handkerchief and uses it to draw a big circle in the air vertically in front of him.*)

    is an eternal raund "O"

(*Left hand up from the elbow, right hand out, broad smile.*)

    of delights.

VOCAL AND PHYSICAL CHARACTERIZATION

Few characters depend so heavily on exactly the right sort of physical characterization as does Lord Foppington. It is easy to make the audience laugh by strutting about in an absurd manner, but quite difficult to capture the precision and grace that make the character believable and turn him from a mere buffoon into someone genuinely comic.

Begin with the posture. The shoulders and head are tilted well back; the chest is out. There will be a certain rigidity in the stance above the waist, for the legs do all the work of walking, and the impact of the walk is absorbed in the knees and the ankles. From the waist up, Lord Foppington appears almost to glide.

The expression on the face is one of deeply ingrained snobbery. The eyebrows are slightly up, the nose is at such an angle as to suggest some unpleasant smell in the surroundings (which is escaped from by frequent use of the snuffbox). The eyelids are not fully open and probably blink rather frequently, showing that the character is much more absorbed in holding himself properly and otherwise attending to his own appearance than in watching what is going on around him.

The actor should work with both the feet and the hands. Lord Foppington walks as if he were dancing a minuet. He points the toe in the direction his foot is to land and lands the toe rather than the heel. A favorite stance is to have one foot at right angles to the other, the heel of one just touching the arch of the other. The knee of that leg angled away from the center of the body the most would be bent enough so that the pose is noticeably attractive. Each step is calculated as carefully as if it had been rehearsed, though Lord Foppington has acquired through long practice enough grace so that he need no longer rehearse anything.

A great deal of fluidity in the wrists is important. The fingers and the palm of the hand should be able to be very active without any change in the position of the elbow. As he talks, Lord Foppington will have his fingers almost continuously in motion, adding to the frilly effect of his general appearance. Probably the hands will never fall below the level of the elbows. They will be up for the sake of the pose, to hold the snuffbox, to hold the gloves, and to hold the handkerchief. The handkerchief may be twirled elaborately from time to time, to give the character additional flourishes.

All in all, Lord Foppington should look as if he is used to wearing fine clothes and an elaborate wig and is proudly showing them off. He will assume that admiring eyes are always on him, and will attempt never to disappoint those eyes.

The voice is centered as far forward in the face as possible, in keeping with the superficial quality of the character as a whole. A stiff upper lip will give a certain crispness to the sound, and an avoidance of any sound through the nose, so that the entire resonance falls below the nasal passages and above the throat, will add to the crispness of the effect. Excessive use of the lips in shaping the words so that they take on an artificial sound is also appropriate. In fact, the lower front of the face is extraordinarily active, while the back of the mouth, the throat, the chest, and even the diaphragm play relatively little part in producing the sound.

Just as he moves in carefully designed flourishes, Lord Foppington speaks in them as well. Each phrase has a musical lilt and a slight rise of inflection at its end. The overall effect, however, is quite dogmatic, so that the general impression is of a falling rather than a rising inflection. The sound of his words is affected, as indicated by the broad "a" instead of the "o" in the dialogue.

This results partly from lifting the sound toward the roof of the mouth instead of projecting it directly forward.

Finally, Lord Foppington's every sound, every gesture, every thought must seem completely effortless, as if he were totally uninvolved in, uncommitted to, all things that he is doing. He is a man to whom life offers no threats, since he is so above it, so remote from it, that it cannot possibly concern him.

THE ANCIENT SNUFFING RITUAL

NOTE: The time-honored Snuffing Ritual below was originated by eminent snuffers of the 18th century. This is the authentic version, handed down through generations here and abroad. As in the mixing of an authentic dry martini, several schools of thought exist as to how to snuff in these modern times. Here is the fine old method, somewhat elaborate, but still in use among British nobility today:

1. Take your snuffbox in your right hand. Flourish it discreetly, to call attention to this precious possession.
2. Pass your snuffbox from your right to your left hand, again with a discreet flourish.
3. Tap the top of your snuffbox three times with the forefinger of your right hand, to settle the snuff and center it in the midst of the inner box.
4. Open the snuffbox with caution and reverence, lifting the lid in such a way that not a grain of the precious contents is spilled.
5. Take up a pinch of the snuff with a flourish, between your right thumb and forefinger.
6. Hold the snuff a moment or two between the fingers, before carrying it to the nostrils.
7. Put the pinch of snuff to your own nose, first to the right nostril, then to the left.
8. Sniff in the snuff with precision at both nostrils, but without any grimace. Accomplished snuffers do not sneeze.
9. Pass your snuffbox to those with you, first the ladies, then the gentlemen, and receive it back when it has gone the rounds.
10. Gather up the snuff in the box by striking the side with the middle and forefinger of your right hand.
11. Carefully close your snuffbox, and put it away.

MY LAST DUCHESS

(by Robert Browning)

Scene: Ferrara
That's my last Duchess painted on the wall,
Looking as if she were alive. I call
That piece a wonder, now: Frà Pandolf's hands
Worked busily a day, and there she stands.
Will't please you sit and look at her? I said
"Frà Pandolf" by design, for never read
Strangers like you that pictured countenance,
The depth and passion of its earnest glance,
But to myself they turned (since none puts by
The curtain I have drawn for you, but I)
And seemed as they would ask me, if they durst,
How such a glance came there; so, not the first
Are you to turn and ask thus. Sir, 'twas not
Her husband's presence only, called that spot
Of joy into the Duchess' cheek: perhaps
Frà Pandolf chanced to say, "Her mantle laps
Over my Lady's wrist too much," or "Paint
Must never hope to reproduce the faint
Half-flush that dies along her throat"; such stuff
Was courtesy, she thought, and cause enough
For calling up that spot of joy. She had
A heart—how shall I say?—too soon made glad,
Too easily impressed; she liked whate'er
She looked on, and her looks went everywhere.
Sir, 'twas all one! My favor at her breast,
The dropping of the daylight in the West,
The bough of cherries some officious fool
Broke in the orchard for her, the white mule
She rode with round the terrace—all and each
Would draw from her alike the approving speech,
Or blush, at least. She thanked men—good; but thanked
Somehow—I know not how—as if she ranked
My gift of a nine-hundred-years-old name
With anybody's gift. Who'd stoop to blame
This sort of trifling? Even had you skill

> In speech (which I have not) to make your will
> Quite clear to such an one, and say, "Just this
> Or that in you disgusts me; here you miss,
> Or there exceed the mark"—and if she let
> Herself be lessoned so, nor plainly set
> Her wits to yours, forsooth, and made excuse
> —E'en then would be some stooping, and I choose
> Never to stoop. Oh, sir, she smiled, no doubt,
> Whene'er I passed her; but who passed without
> Much the same smile? This grew; I gave commands;
> Then all smiles stopped together. There she stands
> As if alive. Will't please you rise? We'll meet
> The company below, then. I repeat,
> The Count your master's known munificence
> Is ample warrant that no just pretence
> Of mine for dowry will be disallowed;
> Though his fair daughter's self, as I avowed
> At starting, is my object. Nay, we'll go
> Together down, sir! Notice Neptune, though,
> Taming a sea-horse, thought a rarity,
> Which Claus of Innsbruck cast in bronze for me!

COMMENTARY

The Poetic Form

Robert Browning, one of the greatest poets of the 19th century, was famous for his development of the poetic form called the dramatic monologue. Though his poems in this form are meant to be read rather than performed, they are dramatically more successful than Browning's plays, perhaps because the poet was more skillful at depicting a single character than at imagining action between characters.

The purpose of the dramatic monologue, of which "My Last Duchess" is perhaps the best-known example, is to suggest through a short incident from a speaker's life, and from the way in which the speaker talks, the nature of that speaker's whole life. Browning has concentrated in this monologue a great deal of information about the Duke's personality, his outlook on life, and his relationship with his former wife, as we shall see. He has also given the Duke a style of speech that is built out of a number of poetic devices. The poem is in couplets (pairs of rhyming lines), but the casual effect of the word arrangement so de-emphasizes the rhymes that they almost pass unnoticed. Very seldom does the speaker pause at the end of a line. Often, too, he stresses words that the iambic pentameter meter would normally leave unstressed. Notice this effect in the scanning of the first line. Read in strict iambic rhythm, it scans thus:

> That's mý / last Dú / chess paínt / ed oń / the waĺl,

Allowing the words to fall together in their natural rhythm, it scans like this:

> Thát's mў / last Dú / chess paínt / ed oń / the waĺl,

Thus, by irregularities both within the

lines and in the length of the phrase with respect to the length of the line, Browning has created a casual tone that is further reinforced by the Duke's use of contractions, and by the frequent sense that he is groping for his phrases and responding to the immediacy of the situation as well as to the past events he is narrating.

We have already noted some of these characteristics in discussing Hamlet's soliloquy. If you compare the Duke's speech rhythms with Hamlet's, however, you will find them very different. The Duke is capable of a lengthier, more involuted thought from a grammatical point of view than Hamlet is, whereas Hamlet's words are much more variable in their emotional implications. Hamlet invites the actor to a much greater variety of tempo changes and tone colorings than does the Duke, whose speech is that of a man whose values have been determined once and for all.

In order to respond to this poem's particular kind of power, one must first understand the technique of dramatic irony as it applies to poetry. The poet creates a character whose point of view and values are quite different from his own, and by allowing the character to reveal those qualities of which the poet is critical, invites the reader to see them as the poet sees them. Thus the poet speaks to his audience indirectly through the character he creates. In order to convey the poet's message, the actor must make the character as convincing and detailed as possible, first making sure that all the qualities of his characterization are implied in the poem.

THE CHARACTER

The Duke of Ferrara is a man who has learned to live entirely without love. He treats the people who are close to him exactly as he treats his possessions, and he becomes exasperated with them if they insist on leading independent lives. As a person, he is icily cold and probably never loses his steady politeness, which conceals immense brutality. He is remote, almost god-like in his attitude, looking down as it were on the activities of his fellow-creatures. He thinks in terms of subtle details, of suggestive phrases, rather than of complete summaries or total situations. His awareness of detail is like that of a fine artist except that it lacks the sense of human values that an artist must have. His presence is commanding and takes for granted in those about him subservience to his superior station in life. He is casual about brutality because he lives at a time in which brutality is taken for granted as a part of everyday life. It is easily expressed when and where the Duke happens to think it is needed, and at other times he doesn't give it a second thought.

To understand the Duke more fully, we must understand a few things about the Italian Renaissance, at least as Browning himself understood it and portrayed it. It was a time of great beauty and great violence. Probably more great painting and sculpture was created in a few Italian cities during the 14th through 16th centuries than has been created throughout the entire world since that time. The Catholic Church, which had dominated men's minds completely throughout the Middle Ages, was beginning to lose the exclusiveness of its control, and a great deal of interest in secular matters was beginning to develop. As the political power of the church was reduced and the political power of great nobles was increased proportionately, an increasing number of godless men dominated the lives of the common people, who had recourse to no unified national authority. As a consequence there were many places in Italy during that time in which it could truly be said that art was prized far more highly than either religion or human life. This characteristic of the time is reflected in the fact that the Duke obviously prizes the portrait of his ex-wife far more than he ever prized the woman herself. His casualness about her death and the incidents that led up to it, as well as his pride in his own noble position, also reflect the spirit of the times.

The Poem

The situation, briefly, is as follows. The Duke of Ferrara, a widower, is chatting with the emissary from another noble family about his prospective marriage with a member of that family. As a demonstration of his expectations in the forthcoming marriage he discusses with the emissary his former marriage, via the portrait of his most recent Duchess.

There are three figures in the scene, each of whom holds our interest. There is first of all the Duke himself, whom we have already discussed. Second is the portrait of the Duchess, looking as if she were alive, with the faint flush of joy in her cheek. She is the very antithesis of the Duke, the more so because now that she lives only in a painting, the joy in her face can never leave it. As we imagine her presence, the depth and passion of her glance will give the lie to everything the Duke stands for.

Third is the Duke's silent companion, the emissary. How does this man respond to what the Duke is saying? Is he terrified? Does he share the Duke's contempt for a woman who would dare to smile upon the artist who painted her? Is he thinking, perhaps, only of his mission? We shall never know, for it is natural that he remain silent while the Duke speaks; it is not his place to give expression to any feelings he might have; and if he is efficient in his job, if he is the unthinking servant that is most desirable in such a position, it is most likely that he does not have any such feelings.

Looking at the painting, the Duke recalls again his former wife. It is with satisfaction rather than grief—satisfaction because now that she is nothing more than a portrait she can give him no further trouble. She has become a permanent possession of his and does not stand in the way of his obtaining another one, her successor. In fact, it is the painting, rather than the Duchess, that occupies his thoughts at first. It is a masterpiece, and he is proud of it.

Yet it is not Frà Pandolf's genius that most concerns the Duke, it is his ability to call forth in the Duchess emotions, or at least reactions, that the Duke feels should be reserved for himself. Perhaps this is why he keeps the picture behind a curtain and allows it to be seen only in his presence. Even strangers are shocked by its expression and cast a curious glance at the Duke, wondering why he ever permitted such a thing.

The Duke is titillating the emissary's curiosity. He wants to show that he is aware of the unacceptable feelings the picture portrays, and at the same time he wants to keep his listener in suspense as to what he did about them. His firmness in dealing with the situation will prove a feather in his cap, the more so if he has first made his listener very interested in the affair.

The Duke is a man who expects to be loved to the exclusion of everyone and everything else. His wife's delight in a sunset, her joy in the beauty of a bough of cherries, her favorite mule, anything in which she found delight, became the object of his jealousy. One can imagine that the Duchess may really have loved her husband at first, for she had a very loving nature, but that as his jealousy increased he became less bearable to live with, until finally she could not feel the love he demanded.

Feeling increasingly that the Duchess did not love him more than others with whom she associated, the Duke's pride was hurt. Was not he of better birth than others? He could trace his family back nine hundred years. It was beneath him to concern himself with his wife's trifling. Suppose that he had the skill to reprimand her, and that she understood him and changed her behavior, even such a reprimand would be beneath his dignity. Because the Duchess responded openly and easily to others, because she was pleased at the casual flattery of a man, even though he might be an artist and therefore her social inferior, the Duke became incensed at her. He felt that as the wife of a great nobleman she should pay more respect to her position in life. She had offended his pride.

Having been brought up to believe himself superior to everyone else, the Duke could never become close to anyone emotionally. Pride dictated all his personal relations. As his feeling that she did not respect him grew, the Duke finally began to feel that it was necessary to take some action. We can only imagine what commands he gave; possibly he locked his wife up in her room and kept her away from the things she loved until she had nothing left to live for and consequently died; possibly he had her murdered.

The Duchess was a problem for the Duke. He did not love her, because he did not know what love was. But he wanted her to love him, and when she did not he wanted only to be rid of her. Her death was a victory for him. He is pleased, now, that he has her picture only, that she can no longer cause him any more concern than the nagging annoyance he feels when he remembers that the spot of joy upon her cheek was not aroused by him.

The story of the Duke's former marriage now completed, he draws the curtain before the painting and urges his guest to rise and go with him to join his other guests. He tells the emissary, as a hint, that the Count whose daughter he intends to marry is known to be so generous that he is likely to provide any reasonable dowry the Duke may suggest. The Duke hastens to add, without sincerity, of course, that it is not the money he is interested in, but the girl. Having been given so chilling a picture of his previous marriage, we shudder to think what will become of this poor Count's daughter. But the Duke has, through his narrative, given the emissary a complete picture of what he will expect in marriage.

The emissary's natural deference to his social superior causes him to wait for the Duke to lead the way downstairs. With a gesture of artificial camaraderie, the Duke throws his arm about his guest's shoulder, saying, "Nay, we'll go together down, sir." For a moment, though, they pause before the bronze statue of Neptune taming a seahorse. How perfectly the statue symbolizes the marriage that is about to take place, for the Duke is aloof as a god, and regards a wife as an inferior creature who must be kept under his thumb. At any rate, the incident gives the Duke an additional chance to show how proud he is of the works he has commissioned artists to produce for him.

Two lives have been laid side by side for us in this monologue. Our sympathy has been stirred for the Duchess who, with her natural delight in many facets of life, brought tragedy upon herself. The other is the Duke, whose power makes him immune from such tragedy, but who, though he can enjoy power and beauty, will never know genuine love.

MY LAST DUCHESS

(*The stage is set with two chairs, C, about one foot apart. They are placed in front of an imaginary portrait, which is located DC. They should be about five to ten feet upstage of it. The Duke enters, UR, allows his companion to pass in front of him into the room, then crosses DC and pulls an imaginary cord to reveal the portrait of the Duchess. He regards it for a moment, then takes a few steps backwards. Finally, he turns to his companion, who is now standing at his right, and gestures toward the painting with his left hand.)*

    That's my last Duchess painted on the wall,
    Looking as if she were alive. I call
    That piece a wonder, now: Frà Pandolf's[1] hands
    Worked busily a day, and there she stands.

(He gestures toward the chair in front of which his companion stands.)

    Will't please you sit and look at her?

(He sits in the chair in front of which he has been standing.)

                     I said
    "Frà Pandolf" by design, for never read
    Strangers like you that pictured countenance,
    The depth and passion of its earnest glance,

(He shifts his gaze from the portrait to his companion, and his tone becomes more personal as he attempts to draw the man more deeply into the situation he is about to describe.)

    But to myself they turned (since none puts by
    The curtain I have drawn for you, but I)
    And seemed as they would ask me,

(Just the slightest hint of a threat in the Duke's voice to remind the emissary of their respective stations in life.)

                     if they durst,

(Looks at the picture again, contemplating it more critically.)

    How such a glance came there;

(Puts his arm around the back of his companion's chair, becoming personable and relaxed again.)

                  so, not the first
    Are you to turn and ask thus.

(He rises, but holds his position in front of the chair, his arms at his sides. He gives special weight to the words "her husband's presence only.")

                  Sir, 'twas not
    Her husband's presence only, called that spot
    Of joy into the Duchess' cheek:

(Walks a couple of steps toward the left, seemingly conjuring up in his mind the scene between Frà Pandolf and his wife.)

                perhaps
    Frà Pandolf chanced to say,

Max Maynard as the Duke of Ferrara: "Then all smiles stopped together."

88 / Scenes to Perform

(*Again faces the portrait and regards it critically.*)

>   "Her mantle laps
> Over my Lady's wrist too much,"

(*Puts his right foot up on the seat of the chair, allows his right arm to rest comfortably on his knee while the hand gives emphasis to his words. The casualness of his tone is meant to underplay Frà Pandolf.*)

>   or, "Paint
> Must never hope to reproduce the faint
> Half-flush that dies along her throat";

(*Puts his foot again on the floor and stands erectly, but not stiffly, dividing his attention between the portrait and the emissary.*)

>   such stuff
> Was courtesy, she thought, and cause enough
> For calling up that spot of joy.

(*His gaze and tone become distant and reflective. His left hand helps him to grope for words by stroking his chin, by allowing its fingers to play in the air, and by giving a sweeping gesture on "everywhere."*)

>   She had
> A heart—how shall I say—too soon made glad,
> Too easily impressed; she liked whate'er
> She looked on, and her looks went everywhere.

(*Sits, gestures toward his companion.*)

> Sir, 'twas all one!

(*Right hand out, about chest level, toward the portrait.*)

>   My favor at her breast,

(*Left hand out farther, about shoulder level, indicating and suggesting the sunset.*)

> The dropping of the daylight in the West,

(*Right hand pantomiming the holding up of a bough of cherries.*)

> The bough of cherries some officious fool
> Broke in the orchard for her,

(*Both hands on knees in a gesture indicating increasing exasperation with what he is describing.*)

>   the white mule
> She rode with round the terrace—

(*Getting his equanimity again, he spreads both hands in the air in a manner intended to suggest his wife's lack of discrimination.*)

                                              all and each
Would draw from her alike the approving speech,
Or blush, at least.

(*Folds his arms in front of him and leans sideways toward the emissary, with a confidential tone.*)

                                  She thanked men—good; but thanked
Somehow—

(*Keeping his arms folded, he waves his left hand in the air in the direction of the emissary.*)

                                I know not how—as if she ranked

(*Claps his left hand onto his arm for emphasis. Speaks with greater emphasis, and a certain amount of restrained annoyance.*)

                   My gift of a nine-hundred-years-old name
With anybody's gift.

(*Keeping his arms folded, he stiffens his back and looks straight at the portrait. He is trying to appear aloof in his anger, as if the behavior of the Duchess has been dismissed as something beneath him.*)

                                  Who'd stoop to blame
This sort of trifling?

(*Extends his arms in front of him, trying to suggest carefully controlled casualness.*)

                                 Even had you skill
In speech (which I have not) to make your will
Quite clear to such an one, and say,

(*Leaving his arms extended, gesturing with them slightly to reinforce the words, he adopts an off-hand manner.*)

                                    "Just this
Or that in you disgusts me; here you miss,
Or there exceed the mark"—

(*Folds his arms again, but this time some of the stiffness of the back is lost. He seems to be musing about what she might have said or done had he spoken to her as indicated above. This is all completely hypothetical as far as he is concerned, and therefore without emotion of any kind.*)

                                  and if she let
Herself be lessoned so, nor plainly set
Her wits to yours, forsooth, and made excuse

(*Keeping his arms folded, he rises slowly while he is speaking.*)

       —E'en then would be some stooping,

(*Turns and faces the emissary. Looks extremely imposing. Still keeps his arms folded. Speaks in a firm, commanding voice.*)

           and I choose
Never to stoop.

(*Puts his foot on the chair seat as before.*)

         Oh, sir, she smiled, no doubt,
Whene'er I passed her;

(*Points the index finger of his right hand at the emissary. His voice again becomes slightly threatening.*)

           but who passed without
Much the same smile?

(*Puts his foot on the floor. Holds his hands at chest level, palm against palm.*)

           This grew;

(*Crosses around behind emissary. Stands with his hands in the same position.*)

          I gave commands;

(*Crosses to right of emissary, so that he stands right next to him, looking down at him.*)

   Then all smiles stopped together.

(*A pause, during which he gradually shifts his gaze from the emissary to the portrait. When he speaks his voice has a distant quality, more distant than at any other time in the poem. The words "as if" are emphasized very, very slightly.*)

           There she stands
As if alive.

(*He extends his left arm out, behind, but above the emissary. His right arm indicates the action of rising and is extended in front of him. His tone changes to one of lightness and sociability, which contrasts greatly with what has just preceded it.*)

         Will't please you rise? We'll meet
The company below, then.

(*Crosses toward UR slowly, the emissary behind him, as he talks.*)

           I repeat,
The Count your master's known munificence[2]
Is ample warrant that no just pretence
Of mine for dowry will be disallowed;

(*Has almost reached the exit, turns so that he stands facing the emissary. Emphasis on the word "self".*)

   Though his fair daughter's self, as I avowed
At starting, is my object.

(*His left arm extended, his left hand beckons to the emissary, who is just beyond arm's length away. His affability increases.*)

         Nay, we'll go
Together down, sir!

(*With his right hand points to a statue imagined to be DR.*)

           Notice Neptune, though,
Taming a sea-horse, thought a rarity,
Which Claus of Innsbruck[3] cast in bronze for me!

(*The above action has been almost parenthetical with the one preceding it. The left arm follows through by clapping the emissary on the back and leading him out.*)

NOTES

[1] *Frà Pandolf,* a fictitious painter who was a monk. ("Frà" means brother.)
[2] *munificence,* great generosity.
[3] *Claus of Innsbruck,* a fictitious sculptor.

VOCAL AND PHYSICAL CHARACTERIZATION

The chief thing the Duke possesses is his dignity, which he never allows to disappear even for a moment. It is as natural for him to be dignified as it is to breathe. And yet, it is extremely important to him that others always be aware of that dignity in its full extent and power. This desire for awareness in others makes him somewhat calculated in the way he behaves. His gestures are slow and economical. His posture is extremely tem of values should not be called into question. One way to prevent its being challenge an ease and lightness that will reinforce the casualness of his tone.

It is important to the Duke that his system of values should not be called into question. One way to prevent its being challenged is to assume that challenge of any kind is either ridiculous or impossible. Because the Duke assumes that everything he says is immediately accepted by others as true, he does not have to make any effort to emphasize his words. Quite the contrary, he gives them an intimate quality he does not really feel, as if to invite the listener to accept everything at face value. A slight rise in pitch at the end of the phrase will help to give this impression.

The Duke's voice may equally well be heavy or light, resonant or breathy; but it must be clear and controlled, without observable emotional effect. The same source of dignity that gives the body its basically controlled quality should serve the voice. Each word is calculated before it is spoken, and then is clearly enunciated. The Duke's speech is not painfully exaggerated; it is, rather, habitually precise.

NOSE SPEECH

(from *Cyrano de Bergerac* by Edmund Rostand,
translated by T. Jefferson Kline)

Oh no, young man, that's really all too short.
One might (good Lord)—oh, many a thing retort—
By varying the tone. Take, say, this pose:
Aggressive: "I, sir, had I such a nose,
I should have had it amputated straight!"
Friendly: "But dunks it not in cup or plate?
Why not have made a special goblet grand?"
Descriptive: "A rock, a peak—a headland!
A headland? Nay, a peninsula, this face!"
Curious: "What is this oblong case?
A scissors box, perhaps, or inkstand?—no?"
Courteous: "You love the sparrows so
That, fatherly, you occupy yourself
Providing for their tiny feet a shelf?"
Truculent: "When you begin to smoke
Do not the vapors from this nose evoke
From neighbors 'round the cry, 'Chimney's a-fire!'?"
Considerate: "Be careful, lest you tire—
So great a weight may nose-first make you fall."
Tender: "Bring me my parasol!
His color fades beneath the sun's hot blows."
Pedantic: "Aristophanes allows
Hippocampelephantocamelos alone
Was known to have such flesh on so much bone."
Cavalier: "Why, friend—this hook in fashion?
How useful it might be to hang our hats on."
Pompous: "No breeze, King Nose, could be expected
To tempt from you a sneeze (North Wind excepted.)"
Dramatic: "The Red Sea when it doth bleed!"
Admiring: "A perfumer's sign, indeed!"
Poetic: "Was this conch for Triton meant?"
Naïve: "When may one view the monument?"
Respectful: "Sir, your praises I intone.
You have, I see, a house that's all your own."
Rustic: "Blimey! That's a nose? Nay, tell 'em

'Tis some giant turnip or dwarfed melon!"
Warlike: "The cavalry, my men, take aim!"
Practical: "Let's have some clever game.
Surely *this* could be the winner's prize!"
Last, like Pyramus, with tearful eyes:
"What trait'rous nose is this which lays to waste
Its master's countenance? He's all outfaced!"
These, sir, but sample what you might have said
Had you some trace of letters in your head.
But of letters, oh most miserable cur,
You have so few, that your biographer
Contents himself with four to make a rule
To measure you: f–o–o–l—fool.
Moreover, were you quick at repartee,
And had before this noble gallery
Been able to address yourself to me
With crazy jest and vulgar pleasantry,
Know that you never would have spoke one half
Of a fourth of the start of one! I laugh
When I lampoon myself with verve enough;
But suffer not from others such vile stuff.

COMMENTARY

The Play

Cyrano de Bergerac was a 17th-century Frenchman who distinguished himself by writing romances, by being such a good swordsman that he is rumored to have put to rout a hundred men single-handedly, and by having an extremely long nose about which he was very sensitive. The 19th-century playwright Edmund Rostand created a drama out of Cyrano's personality that has been a favorite with actors ever since.

The play is a tragi-comedy; that is, it is mostly funny, but it ends unhappily. In the play Cyrano is in love with his cousin Roxane, but because of his ugliness he is afraid to tell her of his love. She confides in him that she is in love with a young soldier named Christian. Christian, it turns out, is a man who is very attractive to look at, but has no gift for language. Cyrano, as an outlet for his passion, persuades Christian to allow him to write his love letters for him. Christian is killed in a battle shortly after he has married Roxane, so that she never learns that he was a blunt simple fellow and continues to dream that he was the romantic soul who has written the beautiful love letters. Roxane goes to live in a convent where, for fifteen years, Cyrano visits her every Saturday and reports to her on the week's happenings in the outside world. After being fatally wounded by an assassin, Cyrano reveals to Roxane inadvertently that he is the author of the love letters and learns that Roxane is able to love him.

The Character

Cyrano is a man of style and action rather than thought. His pride covers a deep feeling of insecurity stemming from the conviction that no woman can ever really love him. Consequently, he takes every opportunity to compensate by winning the admiration of the world for his skill both as a swordsman and as a wit. Cyrano is infatuated with the way he expresses things, but he is at the same time extremely defensive. That is, he feels compelled to make an outward show to disguise his inner torment. He moves and thinks and acts at a very rapid pace in order to escape as much as possible from the pain of having to look into his own soul. He has the energy of those who forever pursue an ideal they cannot hope to satisfy.

The translator has tried to capture the flavor of English speech of the 17th century, and has preserved the rhyme scheme of the original, while reducing the number of accents per line from the six common in French dramatic verse to five, which is typical of English dramatic diction. Cyrano's wit is of the type that expresses itself beautifully in the confines of the regular rhyme scheme and rhythmic pattern he uses. The speaker in Browning's *My Last Duchess* uses exactly the same devices, but the effect is entirely different. He breaks up the line wherever possible, and thinks in units that contrast with the verse pattern, whereas Cyrano thinks in units that preserve it. The Duke of Ferrara speaks allusively and elusively, skirting the central issue; Cyrano drives his point straight home not once, but a score of times. Here is a simple example of the way poets use verse to characterize. The actor should underscore and reinforce in the movement of his voice the way the poet has designed the movement of the line.

THE SCENE

At the beginning of the play an actor, Montfleury, is performing a tragedy in the Hôtel de Bourgogne. Cyrano, who hates the actor, interrupts the performance and drives him from the stage. This offends a vicomte, who insults Cyrano with the words, "Your nose, sir, is rather large." Cyrano tops the insult with a masterful oration, demonstrating to the vicomte that he is completely lacking in wit or he would have thought of any one of a number of possible clever and deflating remarks about the nose, a large sample of which he gives. Cyrano then challenges his adversary to a duel, and while fighting the duel composes a ballade (a poem formed of three stanzas of eight lines each and a refrain of four). He concludes with, "And thus as I end the refrain, thrust home!" and wounds the vicomte, thereby winning the duel.

Now let us examine more carefully Cyrano's nose speech. It is a piece of tremendous variety of characterization, showing Cyrano to be a consummate actor as well as a man of versatile imagination; but it has as a source of unity the fact that it is all designed to overwhelm the vicomte with an avalanche of sarcasm.

The vicomte has expected that on being provoked Cyrano will fly into a rage. He does; but the rage is kept inside him. The explosion that is to come is artfully delayed and released in a series of stages that begins with the retort, continues with the duel, and ends with the thrust home. The effect is like the flame on a lighted fuse working its way toward the explosion. It is far more terrifying than an immediate reaction could have been.

So what we get at the outset is restraint—politeness, if you will. Cyrano seems to be laughing with his adversary about what he might have said. There is just the tiniest hint in his voice of what is to come. During the opening three lines he is gathering his thoughts and his energies for the series of poses that form the body of the speech. The lighter the opening, the more vivid the surprise will be when it comes. Cyrano should seem to be playing a little game with a friend or a child.

Now Cyrano begins to assume a series of personalities. The actor should be cautioned here not to characterize each of them so fully that the underlying figure of Cyrano, and the sarcasm which motivates him, are lost. We should get a suggestion rather than a full statement of each attitude, a suggestion that falls clearly within the range of Cyrano's tone of voice.

The attitude of the aggressive speaker is to walk boldly up to Cyrano and tell him without hesitation that the nose should be amputated. He is a forceful, obnoxious character. In contrast, the friendly speaker is almost shy. He offers his suggestion hesitantly, and punctuates it with nervous laughter. The sarcasm exists only in the absurdity of the figure he presents.

The descriptive speaker steps back from the nose and cocks his head, examining it admiringly. As the image blossoms in his imagination, his enthusiasm grows. He is excited about his discovery. The curious person examines the nose too, but in an entirely different way. He screws up his face and regards it questioningly, almost disapprovingly. He peers at the nose, examining it closely, rather than from a distance. He sees things in terms of the indoors rather than the outdoors, and is probably quite nearsighted.

The courteous person is warm and friendly, praising the owner of the nose for his concern for the sparrows. The truculent person, on the other hand, is rude about what he sees. Though the nose can hardly be called a fire hazard, he prefers to think of it as one. He is rebuking the nose's owner for possessing a thing that will cause distress in the neighborhood.

The considerate person, sarcastic only indirectly, through his absurdity, points out to the owner of the nose that he should be careful and not endanger himself. By contrast, the tender person comes right up to the nose's owner and offers his help. He offers personally to shield the nose from the dangers of the sun.

The pedantic person relates everything to his classical learning. Seeing the nose, a strange object that he cannot place, he searches in his mind for a literary reference to something that he has never seen before. The nose fits the description of a strange mythological beast mentioned by the Greek comic playwright Aristophanes. His joy is great, but it is the joy of a very small and narrow mind. The cavalier person, one who loves good clothes and fine display, marvels, too, at the discovery; but his joy is in finding a new kind of hook to hang his hat on.

The pompous person is condescending to the owner of the nose. He admits that the nose should be big and strong enough to protect itself from catching cold, but then hastens to add that the North Wind might be too strong for it. The dramatic person, on the other hand, is unstinting in his praise. When this nose bleeds, enough blood will flow to make a second Red Sea.

The admiring person is quick to sense the commercial possibilities of the nose. He refers to the type of shop owner's sign, in general use in earlier times, which was a pictorial representation of some characteristic of the product being sold in the shop. The poet's enthusiasm is great, too, but it is of a different kind. For him the nose is the trumpet-like seashell blown by Triton, a lesser deity of the ocean.

The naïve person thinks he sees a monument that has been draped, not yet ready to be shown the public. He is hesitant, unsure of himself, but hopeful of satisfying his great curiosity. In contrast to him, the respectful person identifies immediately what the nose is: it is the owner's house, which he carries about with him. He is one gentleman admiring what belongs to another gentleman, but keeping his distance all the same.

The rustic person sees everything in terms of his own experience. Since he is a farmer, the nose must be a bulky sort of vegetation. The casualness of his tone contrasts neatly with the stiff order issued by the warrior, who commands his men to fire against an enemy mounted on horseback, which is what he takes the nose to be.

The practical man wants to find some function for the nose. He'll use it as a prize in a game. But to Pyramus, the tragic hero, the situation is anything but a game. Pyramus, thinking his beloved Thisbe had been eaten by a lion, killed himself. Here he sees the nose in the guise of the lion laying to waste the rest of the countenance (Thisbe). The humor of the speech reaches a climax in a pun, for "outfaced" not only suggests "conquered" but also the fact that because of the nose most of the face is sticking out, or forward. Pyramus, moreover, is the most dramatic of all the speakers, since he uses an heroic tone of voice appropriate to classical tragedy but completely unrealistic here, a tone that none of the other speakers quite touches.

We have seen Cyrano characterizing a number of possible attacks on himself in terms of the personalities associated with them. All the personalities are exaggerated enough to become unreal, so that the attacks themselves seem unreal, making a mockery of the whole process. This is perhaps the most successful job of turning a speaker's words against himself that one could hope to find anywhere.

Having shown the drawbacks of the vicomte's remark purely as a remark, Cyrano now proceeds to characterize the vicomte himself. He is so lacking in "letters," or learning, that he has not been able to think of anything witty to say. In fact, he has only the four "letters" that spell what he is ("fool"); again Cyrano has punned. Cyrano goes on to assure the vicomte that even had he been able to think of a clever remark, he would not have been able to utter it before Cyrano would have stopped him. Cyrano is quite capable of laughing at himself, but he refuses to take mockery from others.

This speech brilliantly combines pride, wit, and knowledge of human nature to produce a dramatic showpiece that has seldom been equalled. The actor who captures Cyrano's character effectively, and within it succeeds in bringing to life each of the personalities in his little portrait gallery, is assured of success.

NOSE SPEECH

The stage is filled with people, but the only one except Cyrano that need concern us is the Vicomte de Valvert, who stands C. Cyrano is LC. He stands with his arms folded and his head cocked to one side, wearing a plumed hat. He shrugs and speaks coolly, casually.

    Oh no, young man, that's really all too short.
    One might

Opens his arms out, throwing them up. Still very casual.

        (good Lord)—oh, many a thing retort—
    By varying the tone.

Cross DL, hand to chin, thoughtful. Hold onto the word "say."

            Take, say,

Turns to Valvert, pointing index finger of right hand at him.

                this pose:

Faces front. Index finger of left hand is raised in a gesture of defiance. Step forward on left foot, lean into it. Very gruff voice.

98 / Scenes to Perform

Craig North as Cyrano: "Take, say, this pose."

Aggressive: "I, sir, had I such a nose,
I should have had it amputated straight!"

Steps back, two hands up in front of chest, looking timid. Silly smile and nervous laughter. Voice much lighter and more hesitant.

Friendly: "But dunks it not in cup or plate?
Why not have made a special goblet

With right hand, indicates a very tall drinking vessel in the air, running from waist level to head level. Rolls the "r" in "grand." The sound of the word is extended for as long as the gesture.

grand?"

Looks in amazement straight ahead of him. Steps back in awed reaction with each descriptive word. The left hand sketches a peninsula in the air. He has calculated his steps so that he is standing right next to Valvert and can, on the words "this face" look straight at him, forcing his own nose right into Valvert's face.

Descriptive: "A rock, a peak—a headland!
A headland? Nay, a peninsula, this face!"

Bends over, hand to chin, looks as if he is examining something very carefully. His voice is lighter in tone than it was for the descriptive character.

Curious: "What is this oblong case?
A scissors box, perhaps, or inkstand?—no?"

A broad smile, moving DRC rather quickly with a warm, eager expression. On the word "shelf" he traces a straight horizontal line in the air with his left hand.

Courteous: "You love the sparrows so
That, fatherly, you occupy yourself
Providing for their tiny feet a shelf?"

Assuming a gruff tone and stance, he moves quickly toward Valvert, shaking his left fist at him and shouting.

Truculent: "When you begin to smoke
Do not the vapors from this nose evoke
From neighbors 'round the cry, 'Chimney's a-fire!'?"

Puts his hand gently on the back of Valvert's neck. On the words "nose first," pushes his head forward. His tone is very sweet until the words "nose-first," when it becomes jocular.

Considerate: "Be careful, lest you tire—
So great a weight may nose-first make you fall."

Glides DR toward an imaginary companion, gesturing to him to bring a parasol. On the word "fades" faces Valvert and looks at him, shaking his head sadly.

> Tender: "Bring me my parasol!
> His color fades beneath the sun's hot blows."

Turns and smiles at the audience, looking as if he had made a great discovery.

> Pedantic: "Aristophanes allows
> Hippocampelephantocamelos alone
> Was known to have such flesh on so much bone."

Moves to C, using sweeping, superfluous gestures with his hands. On the last phrase, sweeps off his hat, and pantomimes hanging it in the air.

> Cavalier: "Why, friend—this hook in fashion?
> How useful it might be to hang our hats on."

Squashes the hat on his head, sticks his stomach out, and speaks in a deep, overbearing voice, frowning heavily.

> Pompous: "No breeze, King Nose, could be expected
> To tempt from you a sneeze (North Wind excepted)."

Puts his hat over his heart, and takes two giant steps front, left hand out in a dramatic gesture. Voice very loud and resonant.

> Dramatic: "The Red Sea when it doth bleed!"

Holds the hat in the air in the position of a sign for a shop, and leans back from it, looking at it admiringly.

> Admiring: "A perfumer's sign, indeed!"

Puts his hat on the side of his head, holds his chin very high, and looks very serious. The voice has a breathy but highly shaped tone.

> Poetic: "Was this conch for Triton meant?"

He stoops a little, and looks in a different direction, his hands bent at the wrists. He seems to be trying to peek at something.

> Naïve: "When may one view the monument?"

Turns, walks back upstage, looking carefully and thoughtfully at Valvert. Comes to a halt a little behind him, the fingers of one hand tapping rhythmically on his own chest.

> Respectful: "Sir, your praises I intone.
> You have, I see, a house that's all your own."

Puts his hands on his hips, walks in a clomping manner, his feet hitting the floor flatly. He is bent forward a little. Cross to LC. The voice takes on a rustic twang.

> Rustic: "Blimey! That's a nose? Nay, tell 'em
> 'Tis some giant turnip or dwarfed melon!"

Stands at attention, with a salute. Speaks rapidly and with chest tone.

> Warlike: "The cavalry, my men, take aim!"

Takes Valvert by the elbow and leads him DLC. On "this" his hand covers his nose. On "prize" the hand is held palm up in front of Valvert, as if holding the nose.

>Practical: "Let's have some clever game.
>Surely *this* could be the winner's prize!"

Steps away from Valvert, to DL, meditating intensely.

>Last, like Pyramus, with tearful eyes:

Wheels about suddenly, hands up in a gesture of horror. The voice is booming and very resonant, almost singing.

>"What trait'rous nose is this which lays to waste
>It's master's countenance? He's all

Right hand to forehead, palm out. Chin back. Eyes closed.

>>outfaced!"

Crosses nonchalantly in front of Valvert to DR, not looking at him.

>These, sir, but sample what you might have said
>Had you some trace of letters in your head.
>But of letters, oh most miserable cur,
>You have so few, that your biographer
>Contents himself with four to make a rule
>To measure you:

Writes the letters in the air with his right hand.

>>f–o–o–l–

Looks and smiles knowingly, toothily, at Valvert.

>>fool.

Walks toward Valvert slowly at first, but speeding up. His voice is restrained, though angry, at first, but it, too, speeds up and gets louder and angrier, so that he reaches a crescendo at the end of this section and is towering over Valvert, his left hand held threateningly above his head.

>Moreover, were you quick at repartee,
>And had before this noble gallery
>Been able to address yourself to me
>With crazy jest and vulgar pleasantry,
>Know that you never would have spoke one half
>Of a fourth of the start of one!

This next has a deceptive casualness which is really the calm before the storm. Only on the word "others" is the threat of violence really clear. He stands next to Valvert, close enough to be very oppressive to him. His right hand fingers the handle of his sword. His words are bitten off very sharply.

>   I laugh
> When I lampoon myself with verve enough;
> But suffer not from others such vile stuff.

VOCAL AND PHYSICAL CHARACTERIZATION

Cyrano is a man to whom style is extremely important. He is at least as interested in how he says a thing as in what he says. This is because the things he is concerned with in the play are all fairly simple: his love for Roxane, his pride, his sense of inferiority. What makes him fascinating is that he expresses himself with unfailing brilliance on all of these things. Consequently, he will shape each phrase with almost unconscious ease. All of the quotations are thoroughly differentiated and characterized with great subtlety and complete control. The man must be so fully in command of every aspect of his wit, his coordination, and his voice that he can simultaneously fight a duel and compose a ballade, delivering it with perfect dramatic emphasis. No one can hope to perform this scene well unless he works on each phrase individually, getting just exactly the right emphasis and tone quality to sketch in caricature form each character Cyrano has in mind. He must devote just as much attention to each gesture that he uses. His movement must have the intricacy of a ballet dance along with the naturalness of a completely extemporaneous virtuoso display. The gestures should be worked out slowly and carefully, then polished, and then repeated so often that they become habitual and can be done exactly right without any thought whatsoever. When the speech is performed the actor must be thinking only about the effect he is having on the vicomte and the admiring crowd that is watching him. Everything else must have become second nature to him.

PEER GYNT LEAVES SOLVEIG

(from *Peer Gynt* by Henrik Ibsen)

"Round about," said the Boyg; that's how I must go.—My palace has tumbled about my ears! She was so near to me; and now there has risen a wall between us, and all in a moment my joy is gone and everything's ugly. "Round about" —ah, yes; there's no straight road that leads through this from me to her. No straight road? All the same, there might be. If I remember aright, the Bible says something somewhere about repentance—but I've no Bible, and I've forgotten the most of it, and in this forest there's not a thing that will give me guidance. Repent? It might take years to do it before I found the way. And, meanwhile, a life that's empty, ugly, dreary; and in the end from shreds and fragments to try and patch the thing together? One can patch up a broken fiddle, but not a watch-spring. If one tramples on growing things they're spoiled forever.—But, surely, the old witch was lying! I can put all those ugly doings out of my sight! But—can I put them out of my mind? I shall be haunted by lurking memories—of Ingrid—of those three girls upon the hillside. Will they come, too, and jeer and threaten, and beg of me to hold them closely or lift them tenderly at arms' length? It's no use! Were my arms as long as fir-trees' stems or pine-trees' branches, I should be holding *her* too near to set her down again unsullied. I must find some way round about, without a thought of gain or loss; some way to free me from such thoughts and shut them from my mind forever. (*Takes a few steps toward the hut, then stops.*) But—go in now? Disgraced and soiled? With all these Troll-folk at my heels? Speak, and yet not tell all? Confess, and still be hiding something from her? (*Throws away his axe.*) No, no—to go and meet her now, such as I am, were sacrilege.

COMMENTARY

The Play

One of the characteristics that accompanied the culmination of the Industrial Revolution during the 19th century was a loss of ancient values and a tendency to manufacture one's own code of ethics, often tailor-made to fit one's business needs. Great industrial leaders who found they could increase their profits by ill treatment of laborers rationalized such treatment with a pretense of piety and charity. As these men were among the leaders of society, the result was a tendency to replace genuine, time-worn ethical values with hypocritical ones.

Perhaps the playwright who most effectively dramatized the moral problems that resulted from this situation was the Norwegian Henrik Ibsen. In play after play he catalogued the different ways in which man was corrupted by social standards that were not in accord with his inner needs.

Peer Gynt, one of Ibsen's earlier plays, traces the development of a man who allows his standard of values to grow out of what suits the convenience of the moment, rather than out of something more deeply rooted in the past, or even in his own experience. Peer is a poor country boy who, having no moral guidance at home, lives according to his dreams and is clever enough to take advantage of a great many people without ever being seriously troubled by his conscience. Near the beginning of the play, he carries off the bride at a wedding and then deserts her after persuading her that she really loves him better than her prospective husband. Peer is then captured by a group of Trolls (oafish and misshapen creatures once believed to inhabit the Norwegian countryside). The Trolls impress him with their own ethical standards, particularly the maxim, "Troll, to thyself be—enough." This they contrast with the ideal, "Man, to thyself be true." At that point Peer adopts their maxim, and lives according to it for most of the rest of his life. Rather than be true to his inner nature and live according to his conscience, he seeks to do no more than what is sufficient to fulfill his frivolous desires. In every situation he will do only what he must to get by. He recognizes no obligations to anyone other than himself. He becomes, in short, a typical opportunist.

The only thing in Peer Gynt's life that redeems him is his love for Solveig, the peasant girl who falls in love with him and follows him to his home in the woods after he has become an outlaw. Solveig will remain true to Peer for the rest of his life, and it is to her that he will return at the end of it, hoping to find salvation in her love.

THE CHARACTER

The play is very long and covers most of Peer Gynt's life. Roughly the first half of it (which is long enough for a full evening's entertainment) is devoted to his youth. We shall consider his character only during that time. He is a person who acts on impulse and is unable ever to control his impulses. He lives in a world of fantasies about the great and powerful things he would like to be able to do. He is an habitual liar, not so much because he is evil as because he delights in unreality and can't resist the temptation to indulge in it. He is incapable of being a faithful lover because he immediately becomes infatuated with every pretty girl he meets and then quickly grows tired of her. Since he has never achieved anything in life and has lived entirely for his dreams, Peer Gynt has no faith in his ability ever to achieve anything. He is so unrealistic about himself that only in a moment of crisis can he even begin to see himself as he really is.

THE SCENE

One of the girls Peer Gynt seduced during his adventures in the woods after stealing and deserting the bride was called the Woman in Green. She turned out to be the Troll King's daughter, and the Troll King attempted to force Peer to marry her. When Peer tried to escape from the Trolls, he found himself trapped by a strange, formless creature called the Great Boyg, who was in reality one of the Trolls. Peer was surrounded by this creature, and every time he tried to escape from it he ran into an invisible wall. When he cried out, "Let me go," the Boyg replied, "Go round about."

The episode with the Boyg symbolizes the difficulty Peer Gynt has created for himself by his failure to lead an honest life. He can never take the straight road of truth; he must always approach his objectives in a roundabout way.

Soon after his escape from the Boyg, Peer was reunited with Solveig, whom he had met and fallen in love with before he had stolen the bride. Despite her knowledge of his bad behavior, she came to the woods to live with him, promising always to love him and to be faithful to him; and Peer felt that at last he had found someone worth living for. But the beauty of this love was poisoned when the Woman in Green, now turned into a shriveled old hag with an ugly child, visited him and tried to reclaim him. She told Peer that he was the father of the child and that she would always haunt him because he had deserted her. During his most intimate moments with Solveig she would always be lurking in the shadows, taunting him with the memory of his sin.

As our scene opens, Peer has just been left alone by the Woman in Green, and is considering whether or not he should rejoin Solveig in their little hut. He feels keenly the guilt that stands between him and the happiness that is promised by Solveig. He faces the fact that he is incapable of being honest with her about the past, and therefore can never hope to enjoy the peace and happiness she offers him. He persuades himself that the only alternative is to desert her, and that is what he decides to do.

Let us examine his reasoning more closely. Remembering the Boyg's injunction to "go round about," Peer feels new meaning in those words. Never can he go straight toward something he desires. There will always be a wall separating him from it. The palace that he built in his imagination out of the little hut that Solveig has come to share with him has now been destroyed and made ugly by the Woman in Green.

Peer thinks for a moment about the possibility of repentance. He has heard enough about Christianity to know that such a thing is possible. But he has not been given the strength of a belief that makes it possible for him, and alone in the woods without anyone to turn to, he does not see how he can repent. (He forgets that Solveig always carries with her a prayer book, that she is very religious, and that she could probably show him the way to repentance. He cannot believe in her because he cannot believe in himself.)

Whenever he confronts the possibility of reforming his character, Peer is awed by the enormity of the task. It might take years for him to untangle his life enough so that he can repent. He cannot face the long stretch of emptiness, ugliness, and dreariness he would have to go through in the meantime. And there is so little of substance in his life out of which he might build a better life. A fiddle can be repaired because it is something that is built from pieces. But a watchspring is something that is whole and has its own kind of inner life. Once it is broken it can never be restored to its former state. Growing things cannot be brought back to life after they have been killed. Peer senses that his own inner life, his love of Solveig, has been so shattered by guilt that it can never be brought back to life.

He takes brief refuge in the possibility that the Woman in Green was lying, and is merely trying to persecute him. He considers the possibility of escaping from the sight of her. But then he realizes that he will always be troubled by the memories of the other girls he has seduced, particularly of Ingrid (the bride he stole) and of three cowherd girls that he met after deserting Ingrid. So long as he can be plagued by memories of his wild behavior he is afraid that Solveig's purity will be betrayed. Therefore to make love to her is to sully her, to reduce her in his own mind to someone who is no better than the girls he has seduced without love.

Peer's difficulty is one that was shared by many men in the 19th century who lived and were troubled by what they called the "double standard." They would idealize one woman whom they believed to be purer than any human being ever can be, and they would make love to other women, for whom they had little or no respect. They were unable to develop a healthy relationship between love and sex in their minds, and consequently they could never be quite happy thinking of one they loved as a sexual object. Sometimes such a man would remain a bachelor all his life, carrying in his imagination the ideal of a woman who could never exist and contemptuously making love now and then to someone whom he could only despise. For a moment, Peer considers the possibility of going round about his guilty thoughts, of putting them out of his mind altogether. But quickly realizing that that is not possible, he turns his back on the little hut.

Because he cannot face his problems, Peer decides to run away from them. He wishes to free himself from the sexual desires that corrupt his love but, realizing that he can never do so, decides to protect Solveig from himself. To live with her and not tell her his guilty secrets would be torture. To expect her to love him after he had told them would be unreasonable. If she could not forgive him, she would leave him. If she could forgive him, he would feel that she had degraded herself.

Peer ends by condemning himself to a life of lovelessness. Since he cannot face Solveig now, he will never again be able to face any woman whom he really respects. Gradually he will learn to do without love and to avoid the company of women pure enough to remind him that it is possible.

This speech represents the major turning point in Peer's life. It is his last chance to live happily and normally. It is the last time that he is capable of changing his character, the moment that determines what direction his life will take. But more than that, it is a revelation of the tortured loss of love that plagues the man who has forever forsaken his own ideals.

To those living today, Peer's reaction to his own guilt may seem extreme and unnecessary. To the idealists of Peer's own time, it was a common and torturing experience. Few writers have given us a better insight into the quality of that experience than Ibsen has.

PEER GYNT LEAVES SOLVEIG

(*Peer Gynt's hut is located UL. DR is a chopping block with an axe leaning against it, and some wood. Peer stands in the center of the stage looking after the Woman in Green and her child, who have just made their exit DR. He looks out at the audience, musing sadly.*)

"Round about," said the Boyg; that's how I must go.—

(*He turns and looks at the hut, so that his back is partly to the audience.*)

My palace has tumbled about my ears!

(*He takes a few steps toward the hut, then stops abruptly.*)

She was so near to me; and now there has risen a wall between us, and

(*He turns slowly toward DR, the words coming slowly, bitterly.*)

everything's ugly.

(*He walks DR, running the fingers of his left hand through his hair.*)

"Round about."—

(*He stands, looking in the direction he has been walking.*)

ah, yes; there's no straight road that leads through this from me to her.

(*He looks directly out front, musing.*)

No straight road?

(*Turns quickly toward the hut.*)

All the same, there might be.

(*Snaps the fingers of his left hand, trying to recall the passage in the Bible to which he refers.*)

If I remember aright, the Bible says something somewhere about repentance—

(*Hangs his head sadly.*)

But I've no Bible, and I've forgotten the most of it,

(*Turns about desperately, looking up among the trees.*)

and in this forest there's not a thing that will give me guidance.

(*Brings both fists up to his chest, the tightness in the hands showing the tension in him.*)

Repent?

(*He closes his eyes and lets his head drop slightly. There is great intensity behind the word "years."*)

It might take years to do it before I found the way.

(*Keeping his head down and his eyes closed, he opens his hands and lets them drop very slowly to his sides, in rhythm with the last three words.*)

And, meanwhile, a life that's empty, ugly, dreary;

(*Brings his open hands up a little bit, examines them as if contemplating the job of patching the thing together.*)

and in the end from shreds and fragments to try and patch the thing together?

(*Lets the hands drop again. He feels as if the energy were drained out of his body. He shakes his head sadly, profoundly defeated.*)

One can patch up a broken fiddle, but not a watch-spring. If one tramples on growing things they're spoiled forever.—

(*Raises his head quickly, new hope coming into his eyes, quickness and energy coming into his voice.*)

But, surely, the old witch was lying! I can put all those ugly doings

(*Brings his arms up so that they are criss-cross across his chest. Then swings his hands violently out to arms' length on each side of him.*)

out of my sight!

Warren Sheay as Peer Gynt: "If one tramples on growing things they're spoiled forever."

(*Lets the energy drain out of his arms, while still keeping them at a distance, so that the gesture of defiance turns into one of helplessness.*)

But—can I put them out of my mind?

(*Closes his eyes, and raises his head higher, while his arms drop at an angle and seem to trail out behind him.*)

I shall be haunted by lurking memories—of Ingrid—of those three girls upon the hillside. Will they come, too, and jeer and threaten, and beg of me to hold them closely or lift them tenderly at arms' length?

(*Doubles his fists and tenses all the muscles in his arms, bursting with anger at himself.*)

It's no use!

(*Turns toward the hut, extends his arms full-length in front of him, and pantomimes the action of trying to hold Solveig at a distance.*)

Were my arms as long as fir-trees' stems or pine-trees' branches, I should be holding *her* too near to set her down again unsullied.

(*While he is speaking, he walks to the chopping block and picks up the axe, preparing to go inside the hut. His voice is quiet, but forceful and determined.*)

I must find some way round about, without a thought of gain or loss; some way to free me from such thoughts and shut them from my mind forever.

(*Takes a few steps towards the hut, then stops. There is panic and grief in his voice.*)

But—go in now? Disgraced and soiled? With all these Troll-folk at my heels? Speak, and yet not tell all? Confess, and still be hiding something from her?

(*Throws away his axe.*)

No, no—to go and meet her now, such as I am, were sacrilege.

(*Exit, DR.*)

VOCAL AND PHYSICAL CHARACTERIZATION

Peer Gynt is halfway between human being and mythical creature. He believes himself to be capable of superhuman feats, and he has adventures with supernatural creatures. He is young, active, and extremely charming. Most women find him irresistible. He must therefore have the stature and bearing of a fine athlete. Every gesture betrays an indomitable energy.

During this scene Peer is somewhat subdued: he is uncharacteristically sincere, and uncharacteristically deeply troubled. This will put something of a damper on his naturally vital behavior. But it must be only a damper; one must feel the energy underneath—one must see it burst forth here and there.

Because he is a creature of impulse, Peer will tend to move more quickly and more suddenly than most people. He may take a step in one direction and then turn suddenly in another in a way that catches one by surprise.

And even though he is miserable, his charm must show through. That is the one thing he can count on and which he will never drop. He will try to solve all his problems with an ingratiating smile, and that smile will leap to his face here and there in this scene as if Peer hoped that with it he could make his problems magically vanish. This will help the audience realize that Peer doesn't quite believe he is in trouble, that he is not used to having a problem that won't go away simply because he wishes it to.

The voice must indicate that Peer is used to having his own way emotionally. It has some of the characteristics of a child's voice, for Peer has never grown up. When he has a problem he cannot solve, he will either run away from it or throw a temper tantrum. When he meets someone he likes he will immediately become friendly with that person, much as a child does. There is no reserve about him, no restraint of any kind. His voice can switch from joy to misery in a second. It is also the voice of one who refuses to take life seriously, and whose emotions have little depth.

These qualities may be achieved by producing the tone largely in the head, not giving it too much support, and giving the inflections an exaggerated, unreal quality, suggesting a spirit rather than a person. The actor must be careful, though, not to let Peer become effeminate, for he is very masculine. The voice must be naturally dark and full. Pronunciation of the words must be quick, almost staccato, though with considerable force.

KATHERINA'S OBEDIENCE

(from *The Taming of the Shrew* by William Shakespeare)

A woman moved is like a fountain troubled,
Muddy, ill-seeming, thick, bereft of beauty,
And while it is so, none so dry or thirsty
Will deign to sip, or touch one drop of it.
Thy husband is thy lord, thy life, thy keeper,
Thy head, thy sovereign; one that cares for thee,
And for thy maintenance; commits his body
To painful labour both by sea and land;
To watch the night in storms, the day in cold,
Whilst thou liest warm at home, secure and safe;
And craves no other tribute at thy hands
But love, fair looks, and true obedience—
Too little payment for so great a debt.
Such duty as the subject owes the prince,
Even such a woman oweth to her husband;
And when she is froward, peevish, sullen, sour,
And not obedient to his honest will,
What is she but a foul contending rebel,
And graceless traitor to her loving lord?
I am ashamed that women are so simple
To offer war, where they should kneel for peace;
Or seek for rule, supremacy and sway,
When they are bound to serve, love, and obey.
Why are our bodies soft, and weak, and smooth,
Unapt to toil and trouble in the world,
But that our soft conditions, and our hearts,
Should well agree with our external parts?
Come, come, you froward and unable worms,
My mind hath been as big as one of yours,
My heart as great, my reason haply more,
To bandy word for word, and frown for frown.
But now I see our lances are but straws;
Our strength as weak, our weakness past compare,
That seeming to be most, which we indeed least are.
Then vail your stomachs, for it is no boot,
And place your hands below your husband's foot:

> In token of which duty, if he please,
> My hand is ready; may it do him ease.

COMMENTARY

THE PLAY

The Taming of the Shrew takes place in the Italian town of Padua during the Renaissance. Petruchio, a swaggering, ill-mannered gentleman, arrives in Padua looking for a wife who will make him rich. Katherina, the daughter of a rich man, is so much of a shrew that her father can find no one who is willing to marry her. In order to get her off his hands, he has proclaimed that she must be married before his younger and more peaceful daughter, Bianca, can be. Bianca's suitors set out to find a husband for Katherina, and Petruchio proves to be just their man. They lead him to Katherina, and he decides that whatever the odds he will marry her. He subjects her to so many hardships and indignities that he finally breaks her of her shrewishness and makes of her the ideal wife.

THE CHARACTER

Katherina, always scorned by her father in favor of her younger, more sweet-tempered sister, has increased the bitterness of her temper out of self-defense. Like many obnoxious people, she is really searching for love, but she is unwilling to settle for any love that is conditional. She feels she will never be able to be certain of a man's love until he can accept her in spite of her behavior. The fact that Petruchio will keep trying to tame her no matter what she does will eventually prove to her that he cares about her and will never desert her. Once she is convinced of that, she is willing to give up her shrewishness and love him as few romantic heroines ever could love their husbands.

Kate's feminine instincts are very strong. Once she has abandoned the use of force as a tactic, she immediately realizes that a woman can move her husband by gentleness and adulation. If she is always ready to carry out his command, he will be more likely to give only those commands that are reasonable and reflect an understanding of her desires.

Kate is a woman of indomitable spirit. When Petruchio tames her, he does not break her spirit—he rechannels it. At the end of the play she is a spiritedly devoted wife, a woman who will never cease to enjoy her husband's company.

THE SCENE

This scene occurs at the very end of the play. Petruchio has tamed Katherina. He appears with her at a large banquet, where her reputation as a shrew is well known, but the fact that she has been tamed is not. Petruchio is therefore able to bet two of his friends quite a large sum that his wife will prove more obedient than theirs. Each man then sends, in turn, for his wife. The first two wives send messages that they are busy and will come later. Kate, however, appears promptly at her husband's request, and then brings in the recalcitrant wives and chastises them for their disobedience with the words we have here. Throughout the speech Kate's love for her husband and her sense of wifely duty are clear. Her exhilaration at having discovered a loving and effective way of responding to her husband's request is as important as her genuine moral indignation at the wives who have been rude to their husbands. She speaks with all the passion of the reformed sinner who, having fully experienced sin, is no longer tempted by it. There is not the slightest hint in what she says that she is in any way sorry for having given up her temperamental ways. She knows she has found a better means of obtaining what she desires.

She begins by characterizing the woman who has been guilty of too little restraint: she is like a fountain that has been stirred up so that its waters are muddy. No one will wish to drink from it while it is in that condition. Just so, a woman is not lovable when she is in a bad temper.

Next she tells what a husband means to a woman. He is her lord, in that he is the person to whom she is responsible. He is her life in that she lives only to give him her love. He is her keeper in that he provides her means of livelihood. He is her head, in that he makes the important decisions affecting her life. He is her sovereign in that she owes the same kind of obedience to him that her husband owes to his king. He cares about her personally and provides all the things that she needs in order to live. He goes out into the world suffering danger and hardship, whereas she is always safe and secure at home. All he asks in return for these things are her love, her beauty, and her obedience.

Kate's attitude toward obedience is not easy for us to understand. There is throughout Shakespeare's plays a sense of the importance of order in the universe—an all-encompassing order that extends from the most important things to the most trivial, and that is centered on man's relation to God. Rebellion against a king or a prince is dangerous primarily because it threatens to disturb this order, and in Shakespeare's history plays that danger is constantly felt. It is therefore a moral necessity, rather than a burden, for a man to serve his prince.

When Kate speaks of obedience, therefore, she speaks of it as something that she loves and is proud to possess. Earlier in the play she has learned that obedience means agreeing with her husband no matter how absurd he may be. Once she has learned to understand her husband's whims, obedience becomes meaningful to her. Let us take an example from the play to show how this works.

Pet. Good Lord, how bright and goodly shines the moon!
Kath. The moon! the sun: it is not moonlight now.
Pet. I say it is the moon that shines so bright.
Kath. I know it is the sun that shines so bright.
Pet. Now, by my mother's son, and that's myself,
   It shall be moon, or star, or what I list,
   Or ere I journey to your father's house.

* * * * *

Kath. Forward, I pray, since we have come so far,
   And be it moon, or sun, or what you please:
   And if you please to call it a rush-candle,
   Henceforth I vow it shall be so for me.
Pet. I say it is the moon.
Kath.   I know it is the moon.
Pet. Nay, then you lie; it is the blesséd sun.
Kath. Then, God be bless'd, it is the blesséd sun:
   But sun it is not, when you say it is not;
   And the moon changes even as your mind.
   What you will have it named, even that it is;
   And so it shall be so for Katherine.

The point is that it is far less important whether it is really the moon or the sun that is shining than that husband and wife should live in harmony. When the wife submits to her husband's will, such harmony is easily achieved. When she attempts to assert her own will against his, conflicts result, many of them over trivial matters. In our time there are still vestiges of the kind of feeling we are talking about. In ballroom dancing it is the man who leads, the woman who must follow. Kate is like a woman who has just learned how to dance.

Now perhaps we can better understand

why Kate regards that woman as "simple" who fights with her husband rather than trying to achieve peace by giving in, the woman who seeks the male prerogatives of rule, supremacy, and control. She sees evidence of woman's peaceful nature in her body, which is not built to do a man's work or exert a man's control of things. A woman's soft condition of life and her peaceful nature are in agreement with her physical nature.

Because the women she is addressing have been stubbornly disobedient, they have thereby debased themselves into "unable worms." It is as if, not living up to their human nature, they had not only lost their gracefulness, but descended in the evolutionary scale as well. Kate admits that she, too, has behaved willfully, attempting to match her mind, heart, and reason against her husband's, using words and frowns as weapons. She has found, however, that a woman's weapons prove hopelessly flimsy when they are used in combat with a man, that her strength is weakness compared to his, and her weakness, by the standards he sets, so great that there is no measuring it. As a result of such combat with a man, a woman finds that the very qualities she thought she had in greatest abundance (those needed to help her triumph over him) are the ones that she has the least of. (To rephrase the line for greater clarity: "Seeming to be most that thing which we indeed least are.")

Realizing her inferiority, what should a woman do? Drop her pride (for she can hope to gain nothing from it) and kneel before her husband, placing her hands at his feet. To show the great sincerity with which she speaks, Kate now turns to her husband and offers her submission, hoping to give him ease.

We can see the victory that Kate has won when, as a result of her speech, Petruchio happily cries, "Come on and kiss me, Kate."

KATHERINA'S OBEDIENCE

(*The scene is in Lucentio's house in Padua. There are tables placed around the stage, at which several people are banqueting. Petruchio stands DR, having just told Kate to inform the other women present of their duty to their husbands. Bianca and Widow, who, having been summoned by their husbands, have failed to appear until Kate has brought them in herself, stand DRC. Kate, herself, stands C, facing them. Her hands are on her hips, and she scowls at them scornfully.*)

A woman moved is like a fountain troubled,

(*She draws her right hand across in front of her, palm down, trying to suggest the muddiness of the water.*)

Muddy, ill-seeming, thick,

(*Her fingers come up suddenly, so that the palm of her right hand faces the women she addresses.*)

bereft of beauty,

(*Both hands out, palms up, about chest level.*)

And while it is so, none so dry or thirsty
Will deign to sip, or touch

(*Index finger of right hand up, emphasizing "one."*)

                              one drop of it.

(*Right arm extended full length toward Petruchio, palm up.*)

    Thy husband is thy lord, thy life, thy keeper,

(*Raise the right hand slowly, so that it points increasingly upward, suggesting the loftiness of the idea, but not specifically pointing to the head.*)

    Thy head, thy sovereign;

(*Hands lightly clasped together just above the waist and held in toward the body.*)

                          one that cares for thee,
    And for thy maintenance;

(*Arms extended out from the elbows only, palms up, fairly tense to suggest the intensity of the husband's commitment.*)

                          commits his body
    To painful labour both by sea and land;

(*It is important not to pantomime what the words suggest here, but rather to reflect the feeling of increasing sense of commitment by extending the hands farther from the body with each phrase.*)

    To watch the night in storms, the day in cold,

(*To remind the other wives that she is speaking about them, she points the index finger of her right hand directly toward them, while retracting the left arm slightly toward her body.*)

    Whilst thou liest warm at home,

(*The hands relax, the palms face each other.*)

                                secure and safe;

(*Again clasping her hands in front of her, Kate attempts to portray the qualities she is describing. Her head shakes slightly on the negatives to reinforce them, and nods slightly on the positives.*)

    And craves no other tribute at thy hands
    But love, fair looks, and true obedience—
    Too little payment for so great a debt.

(*Faces a little more toward the audience. Indicates the "subject" with her right hand out, the "prince" with it raised, both palm up. The action is repeated with the left hand on the following line.*)

    Such duty as the subject owes the prince,
    Even such a woman oweth to her husband;

(*Crosses toward DL, gesturing more forcefully on each of the last four words. Here is her chance to show some of the quality that has dominated her earlier in the play.*)

116 / **Scenes to Perform**

Alice Montague as Katherina: "I am ashamed that women are so simple."

And when she is froward,[1] peevish,[2] sullen, sour,

(*Comes to a stop, head held back a little more than usual.*)

And not obedient to his honest will,

(*Turns suddenly, so that she again faces the women and looks at them accusingly.*)

What is she but a foul contending rebel,
And graceless traitor to her loving lord?

(*Takes two steps forward, and gestures with both hands, palms out, from the center of her body to the sides.*)

I am ashamed that women are so simple

(*Raises her right hand on "war," then opens it out and lets it drop, pointing toward the floor on "kneel."*)

To offer war, where they should kneel for peace;

(*Keeping the elbows down, both arms are raised from the elbows.*)

Or seek for rule, supremacy and sway,[3]

(*The hands open out and the arms relax. The head nods deferentially.*)

When they are bound to serve,

(*Right hand on heart.*)

love,

(*Left arm covering the chest, crossing over the right arm.*)

and obey.

(*Let the arms open out, so that the hands are held with the palms facing the body at about shoulder height.*)

Why are our bodies soft, and weak, and smooth,

(*Hands down and out a little.*)

Unapt to toil and trouble in the world,

(*The tips of the fingers of both hands touch the center of the chest about five inches below the chin.*)

But that our soft conditions and our hearts,

(*Let arms open all the way out so that hands are down at sides, having taken in the whole length of the body with the gesture. The hands are not allowed to droop.*)

Should well agree with our external parts?

(*Both arms extended toward the women about half way. The forcefulness of the impulse will not allow pointing at them with one hand only.*)

Come, come, you froward[1] and unable worms,

(*Again, Kate can show off her former character. The hands move in wide, sweeping gestures, not to indicate the parts of the body referred to, but to suggest her former emotional condition.*)

My mind hath been as big as one of yours,
My heart as great, my reason haply[4] more,
To bandy[5] word for word, and frown for frown.

(*Hands clasped in front of her, she again looks demure and loving. Her head, which has been thrown back, is allowed to drop forward slightly.*)

But now I see our lances are but straws;[6]
Our strength as weak, our weakness past compare,

(*Emphasis is difficult here. "That" should be pronounced forcefully enough so that it means "that thing." "Seeming" should be said strongly enough so that it will contrast with the "are" at the end of the line. "Most" and "least" should be so emphasized that their parallelism and contrast are clear.*)

That seeming to be most, which we indeed least are.

(*Crosses so that she stands directly in front of the women she is addressing. Gesture of dismissal with right hand.*)

Then vail your stomachs,[7]

(*Both hands out for emphasis.*)

for it is no boot,[8]

(*Right hand out and downward, in the direction of Petruchio.*)

And place your hands below your husband's foot:

(*Crosses to Petruchio, offers him her hand.*)

In token of which duty, if he please,
My hand is ready; may it do him ease.

NOTES

[1] *froward,* stubbornly willful.
[2] *peevish,* showing ill humor or impatience.
[3] *sway,* sovereign power or authority.
[4] *haply,* perhaps.
[5] *bandy,* exchange.
[6] *straws,* feeble things.
[7] *vail your stomachs,* subdue your proud or arrogant spirits. (For greater clarity, you may wish to substitute the phrase, "hold your tempers.")
[8] *it is no boot,* it is of no avail or use.

VOCAL AND PHYSICAL CHARACTERIZATION

Kate is unlike many other Shakespearean heroines in that she moves without self-consciousness. Since she has not devoted her life to trying to make herself beautiful in order to attract a man, there is a naturalness and spontaneity in her behavior that few women of her class and time must have known. She is quite used to hitting people and kicking them, so her arms and legs move as easily and with as much control as those of a trained athlete. Though she has undergone a great change of character, Kate has not lost this spontaneous and natural physical behavior. She has the opportunity to contrast her gentleness toward her husband with her anger at her disobedient sisters. Thus she can kneel tenderly to her husband after she has spoken and acted vigorously, almost menacingly toward them. There is some elegance about Kate because she has been brought up among elegant people and loves elegant things. Much more important, however, is her vitality.

The high-pitched voice which is appropriate for many of Shakespeare's ladies in order to suggest their natural submissiveness and gentleness need not be used for Kate, though it is not necessarily out of place. Her voice may be relatively low-pitched. The important thing is a great deal of energy in the sound. This is achieved through proper breath support and variety of inflection. The tone quality should be polished, but should have enough of an edge to remind us that Kate can fight like a tiger-cat when she wants to. At the same time there is daintiness in her which she has kept carefully hidden until now, but which is nevertheless enough to enable her to enact the part of female submissiveness convincingly. Her diction is always crisp and clear.

LADY MACBETH RECEIVES A LETTER FROM HER HUSBAND

(from *Macbeth* by William Shakespeare)

"They met me in the day of success; and I have learned by the perfectest report that they have more in them than mortal knowledge. When I burned in desire to question them further, they made themselves air, into which they vanished. Whiles I stood rapt in the wonder of it, came missives from the King, who all-hailed me Thane of Cawdor, by which title, before, these Weird Sisters saluted me, and referred me to the coming on of time with 'Hail, King that shalt be!' This have I thought good to deliver thee, my dearest partner of greatness, that thou mightst not lose the dues of rejoicing by being ignorant of what greatness is promised thee. Lay it to thy heart, and farewell."

> Glamis thou art, and Cawdor, and shalt be—
> What thou art promised. Yet do I fear thy nature.
> It is too full o' th' milk of human kindness
> To catch the nearest way. Thou wouldst be great;
> Art not without ambition, but without
> The illness should attend it. What thou wouldst highly,
> That wouldst thou holily; wouldst not play false,
> And yet wouldst wrongly win. Thou'ldst have, great Glamis,
> That which cries, "Thus thou must do," if thou have it;
> And that which rather thou dost fear to do
> Than wishest should be undone. Hie thee hither,
> That I may pour my spirits in thine ear
> And chastise with the valour of my tongue
> All that impedes thee from the golden round
> Which fate and metaphysical aid doth seem
> To have thee crown'd withal.

* * * * * *

> The raven himself is hoarse
> That croaks the fatal entrance of Duncan
> Under my battlements. Come, you spirits
> That tend on mortal thoughts, unsex me here,
> And fill me, from the crown to the toe, top-full
> Of direst cruelty! Make thick my blood;

Stop up th' access and passage to remorse,
That no compunctious visitings of nature
Shake my fell purpose nor keep peace between
Th' effect and it! Come to my woman's breasts
And take my milk for gall, you murdering ministers,
Wherever in your sightless substances
You wait on nature's mischief! Come, thick night,
And pall thee in the dunnest smoke of hell,
That my keen knife see not the wound it makes,
Nor heaven peep through the blanket of the dark
To cry, "Hold, hold!"
   (*Enter Macbeth*)
         Great Glamis! worthy Cawdor!
Greater than both, by the all-hail hereafter!
Thy letters have transported me beyond
This ignorant present, and I feel now
The future in the instant.

COMMENTARY

The Play

Macbeth is the study of the effect of illegitimate ambition on a man's character. It is also the study of the interaction between a man seized by such ambition and his wife, who urges him to act on it. While the play deals with battles, kings, and murder, it says a great deal that is applicable to ambitious men in our own day, and to the influence their wives have on them.

During the course of the play, Macbeth, who is originally a good man, or at least an heroic one, becomes progressively committed to murder and corruption. His wife, on the other hand, who appears at first to have nerves of steel to execute her evil intentions, gradually weakens, and is finally driven mad by her guilty feelings.

The play is set in Scotland during the reigns of Duncan and Macbeth in the 11th century. Macbeth, following a battle in which he has fought with great courage, meets three witches, who hail him as "Thane of Glamis, Thane of Cawdor, and King that shalt be." Macbeth is already Thane of Glamis. While he stands in awe of the witches, who mysteriously disappear, a message comes from King Duncan, announcing that because of his great heroism, Macbeth is to be made Thane of Cawdor as well. This coincidence convinces Macbeth that what the witches have said is really true. His wife, who has less faith than her husband in the wisdom of simply letting events take their course, persuades Macbeth to kill the King so that he may succeed to the throne. After Macbeth is King he does so many evil things that a rebellion is raised against him and he is finally killed. Lady Macbeth, whose guilt-ridden mind drives her to madness and sleepwalking, eventually dies, perhaps by suicide.

The Character

Lady Macbeth is one of the most complex and fascinating characters Shakespeare ever created. She has, perhaps more than any other Shakespearean character, come to be identified with the work of a single performer. Sarah Siddons (1755–1831), who has been called the greatest English actress who ever lived, played her in a way that has greatly influenced most actresses who have played the role since. Mrs. Siddons wrote an analysis of Lady Macbeth, some selections from which should help us understand the present scene.

> In this astonishing creature one sees a woman in whose bosom the passion of ambition has almost obliterated all the characteristics of human nature; in whose composition are associated all the subjugating powers of intellect and all the charms and graces of personal beauty. . . . According to my notion, [she] is of that character which I believe is generally allowed to be most captivating to the other sex,—fair, feminine, nay, perhaps, even fragile— . . .
>
> Such a combination only, respectable in energy and strength of mind, and captivating in feminine loveliness, could have composed a charm of such potency as to fascinate the mind of a hero so dauntless, a character so amiable, so honorable as Macbeth, to seduce him to brave all the dangers of the present and all the terrors of a future world. . . .
>
> Lady Macbeth, thus adorned with every fascination of mind and person, enters for the first time, reading a part of one of those portentous letters from her husband. . . . Now vaulting ambition and intrepid daring rekindle in a moment all the splendors of her dark blue eyes. She fatally resolves that Glamis and Cawdor shall be also that which the mysterious agents of the Evil One have promised. She then proceeds to the investigation of her husband's character. . . .
>
> In this development, we find that, though ambitious, he is yet amiable, conscientious, nay pious; and yet of a temper so irresolute and fluctuating, as to require all the efforts, all the excitement, which her uncontrollable spirit, and her unbounded influence over him can perform. . . .

This description seems to deny the impression that Mrs. Siddons actually created in the part, which has been described as "turbulent and inhuman strength of spirit." This apparent contradiction has been resolved by Joseph W. Donohue, Jr., as follows:

> In speaking of the frailty and femininity of Lady Macbeth, Mrs. Siddons is describing her notion of the character as it might exist *before the play begins*. When Lady Macbeth first appears on stage she is already wildly excited by her husband's letter, half-perused, and in the space of a few moments is moved to renounce all human motives and instincts . . . Mrs. Siddons is not writing conventional literary criticism but, on the contrary, describing a private image helpful in creating her role. This "original" character . . . does not dominate in performance. Instead, as every piece of evidence contributes to show, Mrs. Siddons has discovered an initial concept of the character *against* which she can play from the moment she steps on stage. . . . Deliberately assaulting the fortress of her own femininity, Mrs. Siddons's character conquers the natural frailty of womankind in order to gain the monarchy for her spouse.*

To create the impression in her own mind that she has overcome her womanly frailty, Lady Macbeth struggles extremely hard to produce an impression of almost soldier-like firmness of intent. Indeed, her ambition is strong enough so that it conceals from her for a time all other qualities of her personality. She must not, however, be played simply as an evil woman, she must be clearly a basically virtuous person who has been corrupted by excessive ambition.

The relationship between Lady Macbeth and her husband is suggested in their first words to each other in the play:

Macbeth.   My dearest love—
   Duncan comes here tonight.
Lady Macbeth.   And when goes hence?

Clearly they are thinking of their mutual

---
* Joseph W. Donohue, Jr., "Kemble and Mrs. Siddons in *Macbeth*: The Romantic Approach to Tragic Character," *Theatre Notebook,* Winter 1967/8, pp. 66–7, 86.

ambition rather than their love for each other. But whereas Macbeth will later in the play become a hardened murderer, Lady Macbeth cannot suppress her fragile sensitivity. The actress must think of herself first and foremost as feminine and then make a supreme effort to suppress her femininity. That is entirely different from playing a character who has actually succeeded in renouncing her sensitivity.

THE SCENE

As the scene opens, Lady Macbeth is reading the letter from her husband recounting the events we have previously reported. The letter gives us our first clue as to the relationship between husband and wife. Macbeth refers to his lady as his "dearest partner of greatness," showing that he regards her part in his achievements as equal in importance to his own; and he refers to "what greatness is promised thee," suggesting that what gives her most joy in the world is the achievement of a great position in life.

Lady Macbeth's way of reading the letter will show us something further about her character. Remember that she is reading these words for the first time, and that, consequently, they are not "acted" as her later words will be. But as it becomes clearer to her what Macbeth is telling her, her reading probably speeds up and her voice becomes more excited. The word "greatness" should receive particular emphasis.

After putting the letter away, Lady Macbeth takes a moment to react to it. The letter seems to confirm a possibility she has often considered, for she is immediately aware of the difficulties her husband may have in doing what she feels he must do in order to become King. She knows that he must rise to the occasion if he is to fulfill their mutual desires. She does not quite trust the good news that she has received, and feels she must do everything possible to make certain that it comes true. In that moment after she reads the letter two things will happen inside her. She will have an initial reaction of great joy at what is about to happen, and she will crush that reaction with the realization that it is too early to count on success, and that she must make herself ready to do those things that will be required to bring about the event she desires.

Having made up her mind that some effort from her is required, she proceeds to review the situation: "This much has been achieved—this much remains to be achieved." There is great firmness in her "shalt be" as if by saying the words positively she could make them come true. Next she considers what may yet stand in the way of success. It is the character of Macbeth himself: "You are by nature too kind a person to murder the present King, which would be the quickest way of becoming King yourself." That is the literal meaning of what she says, but it is not the full meaning, for she speaks of the "milk of human kindness." "Milk" has feminine connotations that will be used again later in this same speech, as well as elsewhere in the play. Lady Macbeth is afraid that her husband will not be man enough to do what must be done. Both she and her husband think that the ability to act with complete ruthlessness is a male characteristic.

She next considers the conflicting qualities in Macbeth's character. He is ambitious, but he lacks the ruthlessness to realize the object of his ambitions. Lady Macbeth understands well the immoral character of the course she wishes to pursue, for she refers to what is needed as "illness," yet feels that it "should attend." This absolute and ruthless awareness on Lady Macbeth's part must never be ignored. She goes on to say that whatever high honors he may win Macbeth wishes to get by holy, or legitimate, means. But he desires such unholy things as the death of the man who stands in his way. In summary, Macbeth wants results without doing those things necessary to achieve them.

He does not refuse to do evil things because he is satisfied with the way things are, but only because he is afraid of doing them himself.

Having decided that the one thing Macbeth lacks is the resolve to do an evil deed, Lady Macbeth sees that her own task is to persuade him to do it. She wishes him to come home as quickly as possible so she can pour the poison of her thoughts into his ear and condemn with her fearless tongue the thoughts that prevent him from winning the crown ("golden round") that fate and supernatural forces, as represented by the three witches, have promised him.

It is at this point that a messenger enters and informs Lady Macbeth that King Duncan, whom she plans to murder, is on his way in the company of her husband to spend the night in the castle of Macbeth. It is as if some supernatural force were at work, giving Lady Macbeth the very chance she seeks. After the messenger exits, she again addresses the audience, exulting in the news she has just received. She imagines the arrival of Duncan being announced by a raven, a bird that, because of its blackness and its unpleasant, harsh sound, is associated in peoples' minds with misfortune and death. So awful is the fate that awaits Duncan that even the normal cry of the raven is not ominous enough: he is "hoarse" and he "croaks."

Now that Lady Macbeth knows that she must act almost immediately on her desires, she experiences nervous but excited anticipation of what is to come. She addresses the spirits of evil in the universe, those spirits who are willing to listen to thoughts that are "mortal" because they occur to people with murderous intentions. She desires that they take away her womanhood and replace it with "direst cruelty." She wishes her blood made thick because she believes that blood thickened by melancholy will cause gloomy ferocity of disposition. She wishes the means whereby remorse enters a person's mind to be stopped up so that the natural tendency to feel it may not prevent her from accomplishing her evil deed or come between her cruel purpose and its fulfillment. Symbolically, she wishes the milk in her breasts, signifying gentleness, to be replaced by gall, a bitter, greenish fluid associated with rancorous feelings. These spirits, or ministers, that she addresses are presumably surrounding her, able to hear what she says, though she cannot see them, and are merely awaiting a mischievous command before they go into action. She wishes complete darkness to surround what she is about to do, because darkness is thought of as a natural refuge for evil.

To understand what is going through Lady Macbeth's mind at this point, it is well to realize that for people living in her time evil deeds did not occur in isolation from other actions. When a great king was killed, or some other profound evil committed, all of nature took an interest in it. The same kind of conflict between heaven and hell that was associated with the fall of Adam and the story of Job was thought by Elizabethans to accompany all great deeds of evil. Concealed by the darkness of night, evil spirits could roam about the land doing what mischief they chose. There was hope of safety so long as an evil deed was shielded from the light of heaven. But heaven had an interest, too, in what was happening, and at any moment might stop the murderer in his tracks (whether directly or by speaking to him through his conscience was not necessarily clear).

At this point Lady Macbeth has associated herself so completely with the evil deed that she visualizes doing it herself. It is her "keen knife" that will stab Duncan. Thus, when Macbeth enters, she sees him as the mere instrument of her intentions and thus does not waste any words of greeting on him. Nothing shows more clearly the deep understanding that already exists between these two than the way they express their

126 / Scenes to Perform

reunion with each other after Macbeth's long absence: it is entirely in terms of their mutual ambition.

Lady Macbeth has worked herself up to such a pitch of excitement that she addresses her husband not only by the two titles he has already achieved, but also by an implication of the third one. "You will be greater than both hereafter according to the all-hailing the witches have given you," is what she means. She is not only convinced of the success of what she plans, but she also has all the determination that is needed to carry out the plan itself. Because she knows the future, she looks upon the present, which has not yet brought it about, as "ignorant."

Like many of Shakespeare's greatest soliloquies, this one presents in remarkably few words the development of a whole course of thought from its very inception to its final commitment to action. We have seen each idea enter Lady Macbeth's mind and become firmly fixed there. She is a character who literally grows before our eyes in the most fascinating manner. The actress must capture this process so that the audience may feel the excitement of growing evil contained in the words.

LADY MACBETH RECEIVES A LETTER FROM HER HUSBAND

(NOTE: The staging of this scene draws on the information given in the previously cited article by Joseph W. Donohue, Jr., on how Mrs. Siddons performed Lady Macbeth. Sections in parentheses are those in which Mrs. Siddons' interpretation has been preserved and are quoted from the article. Italicized words should be given emphasis. Capitalized words are almost explosive in emphasis.)

Lady Macbeth enters UL, reading the letter, and crosses slowly to C, deeply engrossed in it. As she comes to a stop, her words are heard as coming so much from her experience of reading the letter that we imagine we are hearing her thoughts and have been hearing them all along. (We see "her mind wrought up in high conception of her part, her eye never wandering, never for a moment idle, passion and sentiment continually betraying themselves." Her expression of emotion is so completely palpable that her words become "the accompaniments of her thoughts, scarcely necessary, you would imagine. . . .")

(They met me in the day of success; and I have learned by the *perfectest* report, they have *more* in them than mortal knowledge. When I burned in desire to question them further, they made themselves—*air,* into which they vanished.)

("Her first novelty was a little suspension of the voice, 'they made themselves —air': that is, less astonished at it as a miracle of nature, than attentive to it as a manifestation of the reliance to be built upon their assurances.") The three words emphasized reveal Lady Macbeth's absolute belief in the power of the supernatural spirits. She is almost entering into their realm as she reads the letter, identifying herself so fully with them.

Whiles I stood rapt in the *wonder* of it, came missives[1] from the King, who *all-hailed* me Thane of Cawdor, by which title, *before,* these

Weird Sisters saluted me, and referred me to the coming on of time with, "Hail, *King* that shalt be!"

Lady Macbeth looks up from the letter and takes two steps toward the audience. She seems to be affirming a relationship with the evil spirits that has already begun to form. She breathes deeply, almost triumphantly, and then returns to the letter.

This have I thought good to deliver thee, my dearest partner of *greatness,* that thou mightst not lose the dues of rejoicing by being ignorant of what greatness is *promised* thee. Lay it to thy heart, and farewell.

She looks up, just slightly to the left and above her own eye level, seeming to see the future in the distance. She folds the letter once and holds it in her left hand. There is determination in her voice.

Glamis[2] thou art, and Cawdor,

She flings her right hand behind her at arm's length, palm down, about hip level, as if bringing the future into the past. She maintains her gaze. There is an ("amazing burst of energy upon the words shalt be.") Her determination seems ("as uncontrollable as fate *itself.") She pronounces* shalt be *in an ("exalted prophetic tone, as if the whole future were present to her soul.")*

(and SHALT BE

What thou art *promis'd.*)

Crosses DLC, the fingers of the right hand touching the chest so that the wrist is angled sharply. The eyes now shift their gaze to straight ahead. The voice becomes less exalted, as the practical aspects of the problem are now being examined. The word "fear" is almost contemptuous in sound.

Yet do I—*fear* thy nature.
It is too full o' th' milk of human kindness
To catch the *nearest*[3] way.

The voice rises slightly in volume. It is as if Macbeth were actually present, and she were asserting herself with him. The right hand is now doubled in a fist, almost threatening Macbeth.

Thou wouldst be great;
Art not without ambition, but without
The *illness* should attend it. What thou wouldst highly,
That wouldst thou

She shifts her gaze upward to the place where the evil spirits have been established. The word "holily" is hard, defiant, bitter, and almost questioning whether such a quality should be permissible.

holily;

She looks again at the focal point where Macbeth has been established. The voice is harder, more defiant than earlier, contemptuous of what appears to her to be Macbeth's false logic.

> wouldst not play *false,*
> And yet wouldst *wrongly*—WIN.

The voice rises to an almost singing quality. There is so much strength in Lady Macbeth's voice that it seems by its very power to turn Macbeth's moral position into a weak and helpless thing. She speaks much more rapidly than before. The entire sentence is spoken with one breath.

> Thou'ldst have, great Glamis,
> That which cries, "Thus thou must do," if thou have it;
> And that which rather thou dost *fear* to do
> Than wishest should be unDONE.

(*Her carefully chosen emphases show that Lady Macbeth has appropriated to herself the preternatural power which Macbeth's letter imputes to the weird sisters.*) *In emphasizing "my"* (*the actress takes pains to associate the fateful nature of the witches' predictions with the role Lady Macbeth is to play in bringing them to fruition.*) *She flings both arms out full length toward the Macbeth focal point, and her voice takes on the rough edge suggestive of action rather than reflection.*

> Hie thee hither,
> (That I may pour MY spirits in thine ear
> And chastise with the *valour* of my tongue)
> All that impedes thee from the golden round [4]
> (Which *fate* and metaphysical [5] aid) doth seem
> To have thee crown'd withal.

* * * * * * * *

(*A messenger enters to tell Lady Macbeth that the King is coming that very evening. He reports that the news was had from one who ran on ahead of Macbeth and the King in order to report it. Lady Macbeth asks that the man be attended to and dismisses the messenger.*)

* * * * * * * *

(*The lines beginning "The raven himself . . ." underscore the connection she establishes between the powers of evil and Lady Macbeth's own dark ambitions.*) *She crosses to DC, arriving on the word "fatal," at which she suddenly turns to face the audience, hands doubled into fists held below the hips, elbows bent.*

> (The raven himself is hoarse,
> That croaks the *fatal* entrance of Duncan
> Under *my* battlements.)

To remind us that the figure before us is a woman, not a monster, she chooses this point for her heaviest emphasis. (*In a voice growing stronger in its "murmured mysteriousness," . . . she exhorts her spirits.*) *Her hands reach up toward the spirit focal point, great tension showing in the fingers.*

Lady Macbeth Receives a Letter from Her Husband / 129

(Portrait in oils by George Henry Harlow, courtesy of the Garrick Club.)

Mrs. Siddons as Lady MacBeth:
"Glamis thou art, and Cawdor, and shalt be
What thou art promised."

Come, you spirits
That tend on mortal thoughts,

She pulls her hands in slowly till they come to rest under her breasts, seeming almost to cup them, to suggest the area in which the unsexing must take place.

(unsex me *here*,)
And fill me, from the crown to the toe, top-full
Of *direst* cruelty!

She tightens her hands into fists. She speaks almost through her teeth.

Make thick my blood;
Stop up th' access and passage to remorse,
That no compunctious visitings of nature
Shake MY fell *purpose*

Hands out a little, claw-like, palms toward the audience, as if she were fighting off peace.

nor keep peace between
Th' effect and *it*!

Hands again under the breasts, but this time she leans forward a little and shows her teeth more.

(Come to my WOMAN'S BREASTS,
And take my *milk* for GALL, you murd'ring ministers,)
Wherever in your sightless substances
You wait on nature's mischief.

She steps forward and leans into a gesture of reaching toward Heaven.

Come, thick night,
And pall[6] thee in the *dunnest*[7] smoke of hell,
That my keen *knife* see *not* the wound it makes,
Nor heaven peep through the blanket of the *dark*
To cry, "Hold, hold!"

As Macbeth enters, (instantly re-asserting the dominance Lady Macbeth holds over her husband, she is "loud, triumphant and wild in her air.") He enters UR; she turns to face him, her back to the audience, her arms up, out and wide.

Great Glamis! worthy Cawdor!
Greater than BOTH, by the all-hail hereafter!

Macbeth crosses to C, and she joins him there, grasping his upper arms, holding him in an iron grip, showing steely determination in her wildness, rather than joy.

Thy letters have transported me beyond
This ignorant present, and I feel now
The *future* in the INSTANT.

NOTES

[1] *missives,* letters.
[2] *Glamis,* pronounced "Glams."
[3] *nearest,* shortest.
[4] *round,* crown.
[5] *metaphysical,* supernatural.
[6] *pall,* enshroud.
[7] *dunnest,* darkest.

VOCAL AND PHYSICAL CHARACTERIZATION

Lady Macbeth's voice must have a combination of two things: the power and depth that make the actions she proposes believable to us, and the sensitivity that she is trying to crush but that will ultimately defeat her purposes.

The actress might profitably rehearse the speech with each of these vocal qualities separately before superimposing the one on the other. First of all, make Lady Macbeth a woman of grace and charm, a woman of such apparent gentleness that she will never be suspected of the murder of a king but will, rather, be greeted by the King and his followers as a person of warmth and hospitality.

Second, make her the woman she is in her own mind: a woman of such superhuman evil that no trace of remorse will ever appear in her mind, a monster without any trace of humanity. Deepen the pitch of her voice and give volume and weight to the words. A feeling of relentlessness will be necessary to make such a sound convincing.

Finally, combine the two, superimposing the second on the first, but allowing the first to shine through just enough to allow the audience to sense the irony of what Lady Macbeth is doing to herself. We must learn during this speech not only that Lady Macbeth believes completely in her success, but also that she is bound ultimately to fail. But we must never suspect that she is herself aware of the danger she faces.

Because Lady Macbeth is a member of the nobility she must move with assured grace and elegance. But because she believes she is consorting with evil spirits, she can use melodramatic gestures that are beyond the normal range of noble behavior. In the effort to repress her femininity, she becomes very tense. She also commits her whole body to what she is doing. Thus, as she reaches outward or upward to the spirits whom she calls to her aid, there should be a kind of movement more common to the dancer than the actress—a complete and highly stylized physical involvement.

Much of the tension she feels may be shown in her hands, which may be held, palms upward, fingers tensely curved, grasping at the air. She is not a witch, and she is not trying to cast a magic spell, but if her gestures have something in common with such an action, if they subconsciously remind the audience of the witches they have previously seen, the extent of Lady Macbeth's communion with the supernatural will seem deeper. If this tendency is exaggerated, however, then to the extent that Lady Macbeth does seem a witch, the total effect is lost. She fascinates us because she is a human being who wishes to be supernatural, but cannot.

CLEOPATRA'S DEATH SCENE

(from *Antony and Cleopatra* by William Shakespeare)

Give me my robe, put on my crown. I have
Immortal longings in me. Now no more
The juice of Egypt's grape shall moist this lip.
Yare, yare, good Iras: quick. Methinks I hear
Antony call; I see him rouse himself
To praise my noble act. I hear him mock
The luck of Caesar, which the gods give men
To excuse their after wrath. Husband, I come.
Now to that name my courage prove my title.
I am fire and air; my other elements
I give to baser life. So, have you done?
Come then, and take the last warmth of my lips.
Farewell, kind Charmian—Iras, long farewell.
   (*Kisses them. Iras falls and dies.*)
Have I the aspic in my lips? Dost fall?
If thou and nature can so gently part,
The stroke of death is as a lover's pinch,
Which hurts, and is desired. Dost thou lie still?
If thus thou vanishéd, thou tell'st the world
It is not worth leave-taking.

*   *   *   *   *   *   *

                    This proves me base.
If she first meet the curléd Antony,
He'll make demand of her, and spend that kiss
Which is my heaven to have. Come, thou mortal wretch,
   (*To an asp, which she applies to her breast.*)
With thy sharp teeth this knot intrinsicate
Of life at once untie. Poor venomous fool,
Be angry, and dispatch. O, couldst thou speak,
That I might hear thee call great Caesar ass,
Unpolicied!

*   *   *   *   *   *

        Peace, peace!
Dost thou not see my baby at my breast,
That sucks the nurse asleep?

* * * * * *

As sweet as balm, as soft as air, as gentle—
Oh Antony!—Nay, I will take thee too:
   (*Applying another asp to her arm.*)
What should I stay—

COMMENTARY

THE PLAY

Antony and Cleopatra is one of the greatest of all love stories. Cleopatra, Queen of Egypt, has fallen in love with Marc Antony, one of the triumvirate who has inherited the empire of the assassinated Julius Caesar. Antony's absorption in love is so great that he allows his power to weaken disastrously and finally loses all of it to Octavius Caesar, who defeats him in civil war.

Cleopatra, who has been throughout the play extremely inconsistent, sometimes expressing the tenderest love for Antony, sometimes quarreling with him furiously, has nevertheless loved him without question and completely. When Antony dies, there is nothing left for Cleopatra but to die as well, since if she lives, she will be carried into Rome, the slave of the victorious Caesar.

THE CHARACTER

Cleopatra is emotionally very much a child. She has never been denied anything that she has wanted. She rules her servants totally, and can have them killed on the slightest provocation. Her love for Antony presents a serious problem for her. Because his every whim is unlikely to match hers, because he must attend to his worldly duties, however much he may sacrifice for her, she experiences a great deal of frustration in her love. It is perhaps this more than anything else that makes her love for Antony suddenly become the most important thing she has ever known. She desires to possess him completely, and at the same time to have him dominate her as no one else ever could. During the course of the play, Cleopatra grows from a spoiled child into a person capable of great romantic love and of sacrifice for that love. When Antony dies she has only the desire to join him in heaven; nothing else matters to her, except to preserve her dignity as Queen and to taunt Caesar.

THE SCENE

It is perhaps at the moment of death that a dramatic character is revealed most fully and intensely—all the deepest impulses of the personality seem to make themselves clear, and the last reason for disguise is removed. Cleopatra remains every inch a queen as she confronts the moment of her death. There is not the slightest hint either of fear or horror as she asks her companions, Charmian and Iras, to deck her out in the royal robe and crown. Rather, she is an actress who feels compelled to play out her part in this world to the very end, and thus she seems more conscious of her queenliness than ever before. It is just this consciousness that turns her moment of defeat into victory. Caesar's "luck" is only a temporary thing, which will eventually give way to his downfall. But Cleopatra is going to meet her Antony in heaven, and to take her place beside him for all eternity. No wonder she can taunt Caesar. No wonder she sees her death as making of him an "ass, unpolicied."

All these things pass through Cleopatra's mind as she speaks of her "immortal longings." She means that she wishes to go to her death, which she views rather as a new and greater life. There is about her in addition to queenliness a lover's desire to make haste to be again with her loved one. There is, too, almost a pity for Egypt, which must lose her as she dies: "Now no more the juice of Egypt's grape shall moist this lip." But it is the gentle quickness of desire rather than any kind of sorrow that dominates her: "Yare, yare, good Iras, quick." Her vivid imagination sees Antony waking up in heaven, looking at her with adoring eyes, admiring her nobility as she refuses to become Caesar's slave, and sharing her scorn of Caesar. It is intense love she feels for Antony at this moment—the kind of love that holds the illusion that the two lovers are one as they share the same desires and hopes. And she feels so intensely that Antony's desires are hers that it makes her proud to be his wife. She wants to hear Antony called her husband, and her courage in killing herself will prove her entitled to that privilege.

Feeling thus exalted by her love for Antony and her sense of the beauty of what she is doing, Cleopatra almost seeks to rise into the air. Of the four elements, earth, water, air, and fire, she will shed the heavier two, leaving them behind for the living to deal with. She is becoming the fire and air that will convey her soul up to heaven. Thus death will not even present the threat of transition: she is already becoming the spirit that will soon be released from the body.

When Iras and Charmian have finished arranging her crown and robes, Cleopatra is ready to bid them farewell. Iras, in her grief, has either taken poison or dies of a broken heart, for she collapses as Cleopatra kisses her. Cleopatra's complete lack of fear or horror of death is shown by the fact that Iras' death only reassures her: "The stroke of death is as a lover's pinch, which hurts and is desired." What more apt metaphor could Cleopatra, who is going to meet her lover, have selected! There is also scorn for the world in this moment, for "it is not worth leave-taking."

Suddenly Cleopatra is jealous of Iras. What if she should meet Antony first? The Queen must make haste before it is too late and she can no longer have her lover's first kiss. She turns to the poisonous asp almost as to a baby, applying it to her breast and urging it to take her life. She speaks to it endearingly: "poor venomous fool." Then she glories in the irony that this simple creature has the power to defeat Caesar.

Her last words are those of a mother allowing her child to nurse her into sleep. Shakespeare has miraculously transmuted this most horrible thing, a woman being stung by a poisonous snake and dying, into a scene of the tenderest emotion. As Cleopatra dies, she is completely relaxed, happy, and sure of her love.

In this scene Shakespeare expresses a supreme irony. Death has been transmuted into love, and Cleopatra must play it as a love scene. How intense the dramatic effect will be if the audience can be made to share Cleopatra's feelings as she dies, without ceasing to be aware of what she is really doing. Here is great theatre. It arises out of the playing of one emotional response against another to produce an irony that is not merely understood, but deeply felt with one's whole being.

CLEOPATRA'S DEATH SCENE

(Cleopatra is imprisoned in a Monument. The room is bare except for a chair. Her ladies-in-waiting are present, Iras to the left and Charmian to the right. They are both slightly in front of her, so that as she addresses them, she need not turn away from the audience. She turns to the left, extending her arms to Iras.)

Give me my robe,

(*She turns to the right, extending her arms to Charmian.*)

put on my crown.

(*She opens out her arms to the sides, so as to display her queenliness, and looks slightly toward Heaven, as if anticipating her ascent.*)

I have
Immortal longings in me.

(*She closes her eyes and allows her arms to drop to her sides, as if rejecting the wine of which she speaks.*)

Now no more
The juice of Egypt's grape shall moist this lip.

(*She turns to the left, clapping her hands once on the word "quick", beckoning to Iras to hurry with the robe. During the lines that follow, up to "so, have you done?" Iras places the robe about her shoulders and Charmian places the crown on her head. Cleopatra reacts to this by raising her hands to her shoulders and accepting the robe, then holding her head back so that she can feel the crown settling upon it. If Iras and Charmian are only imagined, she can help the audience to imagine them by these actions. Meanwhile, she is looking toward Heaven, imagining her husband.*)

Yare, yare,[1] good Iras: quick. Methinks I hear
Antony call;

(*Warming to the idea, she extends her arms forward, toward the imagined Antony.*)

I see him rouse himself
To praise my noble act.

(*She tosses her head slightly on the word "mock," showing her contempt for Caesar.*)

I hear him mock
The luck of Caesar, which the gods give men
To excuse their after wrath.[2]

(*Now, feeling less the heroine and more the delicate wife, she retracts her arms into a more delicate pose, the hands bent at the wrists, the elbows much more bent.*)

Husband, I come.

(*She closes her eyes, sensing again the heroic quality of her action.*)

Now to that name my courage prove my title.

(*She suddenly raises her left arm up toward the sky, depicting the rising of her soul toward Heaven.*)

I am fire and air;

(*Her right arm gestures suddenly downward, depicting the shedding of the body by the soul.*)

my other elements
I give to baser life.

(*For a moment she enjoys the feeling of the crown and robe by assuming an even more elegant posture than previously.*)

So, have you done?
Come then, and take the last warmth of my lips.

(*She embraces Charmian.*)

Farewell, kind Charmian—

(*She embraces Iras. Iras falls and dies.*)

Iras, long farewell.

(*Cleopatra steps backward in alarm. She is momentarily frozen with horror and does not move from her position.*)

Have I the aspic[3] in my lips? Dost fall?

(*She kneels beside Iras, gently touching her cheek, loving both Iras' death and the proof Iras gives that death will be easy.*)

If thou and nature can so gently part,
The stroke of death is as a lover's pinch,
Which hurts, and is desired. Dost thou lie still?

(*Without rising, she looks about her defiantly, imagining Caesar and the others whom she hates.*)

If thus thou vanishéd, thou tell'st the world
It is not worth leave-taking.[4]

(*She rises quickly and steps back in haste, losing some of her queenliness.*)

This[5] proves me base.

(*She looks upward, toward the same spot where she had previously imagined Antony in Heaven. Her left hand has come near to her mouth or her cheek in a gesture of alarm.*)

If she first meet the curléd [6] Antony,
He'll make demand of her,[7] and spend that kiss
Which is my heaven to have.

(*She takes the asp from the basket in which it has been placed, to the right of her, holds it in her right hand at some distance at first, then slowly applies it to her left breast much in the manner of a mother fondling a baby.*)

Come, thou mortal [8] wretch,

(*She speaks almost as to a child. She is holding the asp warmly in her right hand, her left hand palmed under it. She looks down, fondly.*)

With thy sharp teeth this knot intrinsicate[9]
Of life at once untie.

(*She has become impatient, and speaks more harshly, but her position remains the same.*)

138 / Scenes to Perform

Robin Resnick as Cleopatra: "Have I the aspic in my lips? Dost fall?"

> Poor venomous fool,
> Be angry, and dispatch.

(*Now she feels the poison entering her body. Ordinarily, the sensation would be painful, but because she desires death so much, Cleopatra does not feel the pain. What she feels is a source of drowsiness entering her breast and spreading very quickly throughout her bloodstream. She makes one last effort of defiance to Caesar.*)

> O, couldst thou speak,
> That I might hear thee call great Caesar ass,
> Unpolicied! [10]

(*She looks down again to the asp. The drowsiness is taking hold of her, and it feels like love. She sits in the chair. She speaks to Charmian, who stands next to her. She is so relaxed that she has lost a little of her queenliness, and becomes more like a child.*)

> Peace, peace!
> Dost thou not see my baby at my breast,
> That sucks the nurse asleep?

(*She looks into the distance. Her eyes will no longer focus. Out of the mist Antony seems to appear.*)

> As sweet as balm, as soft as air, as gentle—
> Oh Antony!—

(*With her last bit of energy, she reaches into the basket and takes another asp, which she applies to her arm.*)

> Nay, I will take thee too:

(*Her last words come very slowly, and merge into slumber. The phrase would be completed with the word "for." Her head rests back gently against the back of the chair. Her arms relax and fall into her lap. Her head lolls to the side, and she is dead.*)

> What should I stay—

NOTES

[1] *yare* (rhymes with "air"), ready, quick.

[2] *which the gods give men/To excuse their after wrath.* The gods give men luck so that they will have an excuse for making them miserable later.

[3] *aspic*, asp (snake). Cleopatra imagines that her lips have given Iras a poisonous snake bite.

[4] *If thus thou vanishéd, thou tell'st the world/It is not worth leave-taking.* If you can die so quickly, you show the world that it is not worth your trouble to say goodbye to it.

[5] *This,* the fact that Iras died first.

[6] *curléd,* curly-headed.

[7] *He'll make demand of her . . . ,* "He will enquire of her concerning me, and kiss her for giving him intelligence." (Samuel Johnson)

[8] *mortal,* deadly.

[9] *intrinsicate,* intricate.

[10] *unpolicied,* without skill in statecraft.

VOCAL AND PHYSICAL CHARACTERIZATION

Cleopatra has two characteristics that must be expressed vocally. One is that she is a queen and accustomed to giving commands which will be immediately obeyed. The other is that she is a wife who wishes to be loved, who wishes to submit to someone very much stronger than she. To combine these two opposing qualities is very difficult indeed. The voice must have great dignity. This will be achieved by a combination of very precise diction and a slight edginess in the voice to give it crispness. Though she is a little girl at heart, Cleopatra must never sound like one. Nor must she sound at all masculine. Her voice must be light and brittle, but firmly controlled. It must have determination in the way it controls and rounds out a phrase, so that though the phrase is never rushed (at least not uncontrollably), it is never hesitant either. In her tenderer moments, Cleopatra's voice may lose some of its edgy quality, rising a little in pitch and becoming somewhat more velvety in tone.

Cleopatra has spent her life being watched by inferiors, and has never questioned the assumption that she is better than everyone else in the world. She is not haughty, because there is no need to be: she maintains her dignity without haughtiness. She is, however, elegant. Every gesture, every movement has the precision a fine dancer would give it. There is never the slightest hint of disorganization in the way she moves, because she is never confused about what she wants or is trying to achieve. Though she may change her desires from moment to moment in some parts of the play, she is always absolutely certain of the desire of a particular moment. Giving the gestures some of the quality of ballet is not out of place, provided the ballet quality does not draw attention to itself excessively. It is extremely important that the actress let each gesture blend smoothly into the next, so that there is graceful continuity throughout the scene.

THE JAILER'S DAUGHTER FALLS IN LOVE WITH A PRINCE

(from *The Two Noble Kinsmen* by John Fletcher
and William Shakespeare)

Why should I love this gentleman? 'Tis odds
He never will desire me; I am base,
My father the mean keeper of his prison,
And he a prince: To marry him is hopeless;
To be his love is witless. Out upon 't!
What pushes are we wenches driven to,
When fifteen once has found us! First, I saw him;
I (seeing) thought he was a goodly man;
He has as much to please a woman in him,
(If he please to bestow it so) as ever
These eyes yet looked on. Next, I pitied him;
And so would any young wench, o' my conscience,
That ever dreamed, or vowed her maidenhood
To a young handsome man; then I loved him,
Extremely loved him, infinitely loved him!
And yet he had a cousin, fair as he too.
But in my heart was Palamon, and there,
Lord, what a turmoil he keeps! To hear him
Sing in an evening, what a heaven it is!
And yet his songs are sad ones. Fairer spoken
Was never gentleman; when I come in
To bring him water in a morning, first
He bows his noble body, then salutes me, thus:
"Fair, gentle maid, good morrow; may thy goodness
Get thee a happy husband!" Once he kissed me.
I loved my lips the better ten days after.
Would he would do so every day! He grieves much,
And me as much to see his misery.
What should I do, to make him know I love him?
For I would fain enjoy him. Say I ventured
To set him free? what says the law then? Thus much
For law, or kindred! I will do it,
And this night, or tomorrow, he shall love me.

COMMENTARY

THE PLAY

The Two Noble Kinsmen was one of the last efforts in which Shakespeare had a hand. It is an uneven play, most of it having been written by John Fletcher, who later, in collaboration with Francis Beaumont, became a fine dramatist, but who had not really found himself as yet in this early collaboration. Based on Chaucer's *Knight's Tale,* the play is a tale of chivalry set in ancient Greece. Palamon and Arcite, while fighting for their native Thebes, are taken prisoners by the Athenians. While in jail they see the beautiful Emilia from their window, and both fall in love with her. Arcite is then released from prison, and though banished from Athens, he returns in disguise to woo the fair Emilia.

Meanwhile, the Jailer's Daughter (who is given no other name) has fallen in love with Palamon, and decides to help him escape. Once free of his prison, the heartless Palamon forgets all about his benefactress and she, deserted, goes mad. All ends happily for her, though, because she recovers her sanity and marries someone suited to her.

Palamon and Arcite joust for the hand of Emilia, and though Arcite is the victor, he is thrown from his horse and fatally wounded. With his last breath he gives Emilia to Palamon.

THE CHARACTER

The scene with which we are concerned is generally conceded to have been written entirely by John Fletcher. The characterization is poorly developed and lacks the subtlety that is usually found in Shakespeare's comic style. This presents us with a number of interesting aesthetic problems. In the first place, it is usually the duty of the actor to reveal those characteristics of his role that are created for him by the playwright. When, however, the characterization is weak, the actor must go beyond the author and create additional qualities out of his own imagination. Before he can do this, the actor must be certain that he has exhausted all the possibilities presented to him by the playwright.

In the second place, the situation is an extremely interesting one dramatically, and can be treated in two quite different ways. The words Fletcher has given us make it possible to play the character either as sympathetic and somewhat tragic or as unsympathetic and farcical. It is difficult not to feel somewhat sorry for a teen-age girl who is hopelessly in love with someone entirely out of her reach. The actress might radiate the joy of new love and make us believe completely in the strength of her feelings. Then we should be sorry for her helplessness to achieve what she desires. Because we live in an age which seeks to obliterate class distinctions between people, we would not think of condemning her for having the audacity to fall in love with a prince in the first place.

The second way of treating the scene is to make the Jailer's Daughter appear so ridiculous that we cannot possibly feel sympathy for her. If we relate the scene to the rest of the play, and to the time in which it was written, we shall see that this is probably what Fletcher had in mind. We know that Palamon is the character for whom the audience must have the greatest sympathy. It is he who will win Emilia in the end—and he will do so through the death of another sympathetic character. Anything that weakens Palamon's moral character will therefore weaken the whole play. We know that Palamon must be very cruel to the Jailer's Daughter, cruel enough to drive her insane. He must do this because it is his only means of escaping from prison. If we can sympathize with this action, we shall not condemn him morally for taking it. Therefore, anything that makes our reaction to the Jailer's Daughter an unsympathetic one will strengthen the play as a whole.

Finally, if we consider the manner in which lower-class characters are always presented in the early part of the 17th century, except when their roles are completely romanticized (as in stories of shepherds and shepherdesses who behave like kings and queens), we shall see that the Jailer's Daughter must be ridiculous. A sympathetic view of a girl in love with someone above her station was often represented on the stage in the 19th century, when the important members of the audience were of the middle class, but never in Shakespeare's day, when they were of the aristocracy. The original audience would have considered the Jailer's Daughter absolutely outrageous for even considering that she might claim the hand of a prince, and would have laughed at her no matter what she might have said.

Therefore, it seems best to play the scene as low comedy. That is, attention must be drawn to the physical peculiarities and behavior of the character rather than toward her feelings. She must be made so absurd that we are not tempted to take her seriously, and she must be made so funny that we find the scene amusing.

The Scene

As the scene opens, the Jailer's Daughter realizes that it is ridiculous for her to love the prince, for he cannot possibly return her feelings. She is questioning her own motivations, as if she had some slight awareness of their absurdity. This can help us to see her infatuation as absurd enough for us to laugh at. She considers the fact that she is baseborn, her father being a commoner, while the object of her affections is one of the noblest men alive. It is impossible that he should marry her, and because of that it would be foolish for her to make love to him. She becomes exasperated because her own nature drives her to such uncontrollable behavior.

Wondering how she could have fallen into her present predicament, she recalls the stages by which it developed. First she was attracted by Palamon's appearance and manner. When he chose to be friendly, he was the most attractive man she had ever seen. Second, she felt sorry for him. Anyone else would have done the same, she reflects. We feel, however, that such pity would scarcely have been aroused for someone who was not as good-looking as Palamon. She had often dreamt of marriage to such a handsome man, as (she assumes) most girls do. We learn from this that what she is suffering from is not love, but intense infatuation, and that she recognizes the fact even as she gives in to it. She calls it love, however, and admits its intensity to be extreme. At the same moment, she cannot help remembering Palamon's handsome cousin Arcite. But she takes this as proof that it was not good looks alone that ensnared her: Palamon was her choice from the very beginning. She is in a turmoil over him as she recalls the beauty of his singing. She is unsubtle enough to be perplexed by the fact that she can enjoy songs that are sad. She is taken, too, with his polite manner of speaking to her, completely missing the irony that what he says to her is meant to indicate his complete lack of any desire for her. She recalls the time when he kissed her, and cherishes the memory, possibly finding in it some basis for hope that he loves her. We, of course, realize that the kiss resulted only from Palamon's frustration at being imprisoned for so long, and merely shows his momentary disregard for her feelings, a disregard he evidently thought better of, since he was enough of a gentleman not to continue his advances to the poor girl. It is his grief, rather than his seductiveness, that has held her affections.

The girl is eager to let Palamon know that she loves him, still clinging to the distant hope that she may thereby enjoy him. Her infatuation is strong enough to make her snap her finger at the law and determine to set him free. She imagines, without any reason for doing so, that he will reward her recklessness with his love.

In this analysis of the Jailer's Daughter, most of what we have said is obvious. The fact is that this character is almost devoid of subtlety. Her moods change merely because the playwright wants them to, not because of some inner necessity that is believably real. Her determination to set Palamon free after she has carefully observed that there is no chance of winning his love is rather inconsistent and suggests that Fletcher was merely seeking a device for getting Palamon out of jail. Nevertheless, he has provided the actress with a situation that is rich in possibilities for the development of a character far more interesting and real than the lines would indicate. In this sense, such a part provides a greater challenge than the work of a finer playwright would.

THE JAILER'S DAUGHTER FALLS IN LOVE WITH A PRINCE

The Jailer's Daughter enters with a mop over her shoulder and a pail of water. She crosses to C, puts the pail down, dips the mop in the pail, and begins to mop the floor RC. The mopping slows down. She stands behind the mop and leans her chin on the handle, both hands clasped at the top of it; then emits a deep sigh.

>   Why should I love this gentleman? 'Tis odds[1]
>   He never will desire me; I am base,[2]

Uses the mop to point offstage R, in the direction of Palamon's cell.

>   My father the mean[3] keeper of his prison,

Holds the mop vertically upward, and on the word "prince" looks up at it adoringly as if it were the prince.

>   And he a prince:

Lets the mop fall onto her shoulder.

>   To marry him is hopeless;

Holds the mop in front of her horizontally with both hands at about chest level.

>   To be his love[4]

Lets go with her right hand so that the mop falls into a vertical position, the end resting on the floor.

>   is witless.

Picks up the mop with both hands and thrusts it forcefully into the pail.

>   Out upon 't![5]

Mops the floor very vigorously, LC. She is angry with herself.

What pushes[6] are we wenches driven to,
When fifteen once has found us!

Slows down her mopping, sighs, stares off into the audience.

First, I saw him;

Trying very hard to make her explanation clear, first she points to herself, then points her finger instructively at the audience, nodding all the while.

I (seeing) thought he was a goodly man;

Still holding the mop vertical with her left hand, she places her right hand over her heart. She speaks romantically.

He has as much to please a woman in him

She nods at the audience, explaining matter-of-factly.

(If he please to bestow it so)

Getting carried away, she gestures outward toward DL with her left hand, letting go of the mop handle.

as ever
These eyes yet looked on.

At about this point the mop handle hits the ground and startles her. She quickly picks it up and puts it in the pail. This time she washes the floor DC, in front of the pail. After a moment of this, she looks dreamily at the audience.

Next, I pitied him;

Becomes again engrossed in her mopping, but gives the audience half her attention while she explains this next.

And so would any young wench, o' my conscience,
That ever dreamed, or vowed her maidenhood [7]
To a young handsome man;

Becomes ecstatic. Looks wide-eyed at the audience. She feels she sees Palamon before her, and his beauty is so radiant that she backs away from him.

then

She sits suddenly across the top of the pail. Her voice is jolted out of its ecstasy and produces an effect quite the opposite of the one she originally intended.

I loved him,

Only momentarily nonplussed, she allows her voice to soar with ecstasy, while remaining seated on the pail.

Extremely loved him, infinitely loved him!

Leans forward a little, again pointing a finger in an attitude of explaining.

And yet he had a cousin, fair as he too.

Right hand to chest. Emphasis on the word "my."

> But in my heart was Palamon, and there,

Leaning her weight on the mop handle, she rises; and her voice reflects more the effort of rising than the ecstasy of which she speaks.

> Lord, what a turmoil [8] he keeps!

Holds the mop up and lets it vibrate with the music of her passion.

> To hear him
> Sing in an evening, what a heaven it is!

Reflects with some surprise on the following fact.

> And yet his songs are sad ones.

Rests the handle of the mop on the floor with the mop end up so that the mop can now play the role of Palamon in her little pantomime. She smiles at the mop flirtatiously.

> Fairer spoken
> Was never gentleman;

Crosses toward DR, as if entering his cell.

> when I come in
> To bring him water in a morning, first

Makes the mop bow to her.

> He bows his noble body,

Curtsies to the mop.

> then salutes me, thus:

Speaks in a deep chesty voice, imitating a man, but certainly not a princely one; for this she would be incapable of.

> "Fair, gentle maid, good morrow; may thy goodness
> Get thee a happy husband!"

Smiles at the audience, obviously pleased with her imitation. Then smiles at the mop, working up to the kiss that is to come.

> Once

Lots of fluttering of eyelashes and related activity.

> he kissed me.

Puckers up, and extending her face forward, gives the mop a very noisy kiss. Then smiles very toothily at the audience and savors the words.

> I loved my lips the better ten days after.

Looks at the mop and waves flirtatiously at it. Then looks dreamily at the audience.

The Jailer's Daughter Falls in Love with a Prince / 147

Carole Brooks as the Jailor's Daughter: "Once he kissed me."

> Would he would do so every day!

Looks again at the mop, realizes it is a mop, and goes back to scrubbing the floor, just upstage of the pail. After a moment of scrubbing, she speaks quite matter-of-factly.

> > He grieves much,
> And me as much to see his misery.

Stops scrubbing and scratches her head.

> What should I do, to make him know I love him?

Throws the mop over her shoulder, picks up the bucket and crosses DC, speaking confidentially to audience.

> For I would fain enjoy him.

Her face lights up with a new idea. She sets down the pail and while she is speaking, prepares to thrust the mop into the pail in order to get it out of her hands. This she accomplishes on the word "free" with enough force to splash water all over herself.

> > Say I ventured
> To set him free?

Looks down at the pail with annoyance. Wipes droplets of water off her face. Frowns.

> > what says the law then?

Snaps the fingers of her right hand.

> > > Thus much
> For law, or kindred! [9] I will do it,

Throws the mop over her shoulder.

> And this night,

Picks up the pail.

> > or tomorrow,

Speaks with great determination, stamping her foot.

> > > he shall love me.

Walks very rapidly off.

NOTES

[1] *'tis odds,* chances are.
[2] *base,* low born.
[3] *mean,* low born.
[4] *love,* "whore" in the original.
[5] *out upon 't,* an expression of general frustration, equivalent of modern "darn it!"
[6] *pushes,* absurd impulses.
[7] *maidenhood,* "maidenhead" in the original.
[8] *turmoil,* "coil" in the original.
[9] *kindred,* she refers to the repercussions her actions may have for her from her family.

VOCAL AND PHYSICAL CHARACTERIZATION

Though Fletcher has given no stage directions for this scene, we have imagined, quite arbitrarily, a situation that will give the actress scope for playing low comedy. Emphasis on the physical element in a personality or action distracts from our awareness of the spirit, and makes us better able to laugh at what is happening. We have imagined that as the girl dreams of her lover she is washing the floor of some part of the jail. Her reflections prevent her from concentrating on what she is doing and she makes a series of mistakes. The resulting slapstick will keep us from worrying about having sympathy for the girl.

Use of such a device means that the actress can be relatively attractive without becoming too sympathetic a character. In fact, she will be much funnier if she is slightly but genuinely seductive as well as ridiculous. Her attractiveness should not, however, carry over into her physical style. She will walk in a flat-footed manner, feet wide apart, putting her full weight on each step that she takes. Her posture will be poor as a result of too much work too early in life. Her stomach will stick out, and her shoulders will be slightly hunched forward. Her head should protrude slightly rather than be carried straight. The muscles in her face should be relaxed, giving her a vacant stare when she is not smiling or frowning, with some flabbiness about the lips.

The voice should have a very heavy-handed sound. It should sound nasal, even in moments of happiness. Sustaining the vowel sounds and allowing the inflection to rise and fall considerably within a given vowel sound will add to the effect. The diction should be clear enough to be understood, but deliberately imprecise, so that any details which might give elegance to the speech are slurred out of existence. Important words should be exaggerated a great deal, almost slammed into. When she is excited, the girl's voice takes on a breathy, overenthusiastic sound.

EVE DECIDES TO EAT THE FRUIT OF THE TREE OF KNOWLEDGE

(from *Paradise Lost* by John Milton)

Great are thy virtues, doubtless, best of fruits,
Though kept from man, and worthy to be admired,
Whose taste, too long forborne, at first assay
Gave elocution to the mute, and taught
The tongue not made for speech to speak thy praise;
Thy praise He also who forbids thy use,
Conceals not from us, naming thee the tree
Of knowledge, knowledge both of good and evil;
Forbids us then to taste, but His forbidding
Commends thee more, while it infers the good
By thee communicated, and our want:
For good unknown sure is not had; or, had
And yet unknown, is as not had at all.
In plain, then, what forbids He but to know,
Forbids us good, forbids us to be wise?
Such prohibitions bind not. But if death
Bind us with after-bands, what profits then
Our inward freedom? In the day we eat
Of this fair fruit, our doom is, we shall die.
How dies the serpent? he hath eaten and lives,
And knows, and speaks, and reasons, and discerns,
Irrational till then. For us alone
Was death invented? or to us denied
This intellectual food, for beasts reserved?
For beasts, it seems; yet that one beast which first
Hath tasted, envies not, but brings with joy
The good befallen him, author unsuspect,
Friendly to man, far from deceit or guile.
What fear I, then? rather, what know to fear
Under this ignorance of good and evil,
Of God and death, of law or penalty?
Here grows the cure of all, this fruit divine,
Fair to the eye, inviting to the taste,
Of virtue to make wise: what hinders then
To reach, and feed at once both body and mind?

(So saying, her rash hand in evil hour
Forth reaching to the fruit, she plucked, she ate:
Earth felt the wound, and nature from her seat,
Sighing through all her works, gave signs of woe,
That all was lost.)

COMMENTARY

The Poem

In the latter part of the 17th century John Milton completed his great poem, *Paradise Lost,* written, as the poem itself says, "to justify the ways of God to man." In it he gave expression to the religious and political philosophy that he had been thinking about during his many years of service to Cromwell's government in England following the Puritan revolution in 1649.

The poem recounts the struggle of Satan against God, first as an angel who, jealous of God's great power, raised a rebellion against Him, and then as the greatest of the fallen angels in Hell, plotting revenge against God by tempting man to the sin of disobedience.

Having cast the rebellious angels out of Heaven, God needed to replace them with other angels. He decided not to allow Heaven to be the scene of any more violence, but rather to create the earth as a testing place for angels. Adam and Eve were created in the Garden of Eden, and a messenger from God told them that they might do whatever they chose in that Paradise so long as they did not eat of the fruit of the Tree of Knowledge. Furthermore, they were warned specifically of the consequences of doing so and told that Satan would try to tempt them to their downfall.

The Character

Milton has given us a few hints earlier in the poem as to how Eve's character may develop. For example, her reaction when she first sees Adam is that he is not as beautiful as the image of herself that she has seen reflected in water. Also, Eve has had a dream in which under the influence of Satan she has been tempted to eat the fruit of the Tree of Knowledge. Finally, on the day on which the fatal deed occurs, Eve has persuaded Adam to allow her to work separately at her gardening, charging him with not trusting her to be alone.

These hints become clearer if we understand that Milton believed that in the natural order of things man owed obedience to God and woman to man. It was natural for Adam to watch over Eve and prevent her from getting into situations in which too much might be demanded of her judgment. It was Eve's pride, particularly her pride in a quality of judgment that she did not have, that led to her disobedience.

When Satan, disguised as a serpent, sees Eve, he is momentarily almost dissuaded from his purpose by her great beauty and apparent innocence. But, having strengthened his resolve, he approaches her with flattery. It is the combination of Eve's weakness for flattery and her inferior judgment that allows her to fall into the logical trap set for her by Satan. He argues that if God wishes to prevent Adam and Eve from eating the fruit of the Tree of Knowledge, it must be because He is afraid that they will gain power equal to His. Satan's reasoning is faulty because it is based on the assumption that God is capable of fear, an assumption that cannot be proved. It also ignores the fact that God created both Eve and the Tree of Knowledge and might easily have avoided creating the latter had He been afraid that it would be used against him.

Eve Decides to Eat the Fruit of the Tree of Knowledge / 153

Satan also offers Eve misleading evidence: he tells her that he has eaten of the fruit, and though death was threatened, he has not died, but has instead gained the power of speech, formerly reserved for man alone. He argues from this evidence that if Eve eats of the fruit despite the prohibition, she will gain powers previously reserved for God alone. Of course the evidence is false, since it is not a serpent who speaks, but Satan, who has assumed the body of a serpent, and who has not eaten of the fruit. These are the arguments that precede the speech we are examining, and that provide the basis on which Eve reasons and acts.

Note that once Satan has presented his arguments, it is Eve who talks herself into the sin she will commit. Though he is the tempter, she is responsible for the action that follows. Because she allows herself to reason without the guidance of Adam, despite the fact that she knows it is proper to seek such guidance; and because she questions the authority and justice of God, who has given her life in the first place and has further given her all the things that she values in life, she is guilty of the sin of aspiring pride.

Milton was deeply concerned with the question of rebellion. He had himself served a government that ruled as the result of the revolution that deposed and executed Charles I of England, and he believed that the rule of that government was just despite the widely held belief that kings, once they gained power, held it under the authority of God. Hence, one of Milton's reasons for writing *Paradise Lost* was that he wanted to examine the conditions under which rebellion was and was not justified. God's creation was a perfect universe in which man might live a totally good life. But, it was argued, if God created man so that it was part of his nature to serve God, there would be no freedom. It was only if man had the power to choose whether to serve God that freedom was possible. Before he had made the choice, the problem of loyalty was a simple one. Rebellion against a just God was unreasonable and punishable by death and damnation. After Adam and Eve had chosen not to serve God, but to eat the fruit of the Tree of Knowledge, and were consequently banished from Paradise, the problem of loyalty was immensely complicated. Men then had to decide whether, in serving authority, they were serving God. If they wished to avoid damnation it was necessary for them to rebel against unjust authority. By this reasoning Milton condemned the rebellion of Satan and of Adam against God, but upheld his own participation in a rebellion against a tyrant.

Eve, when she decides to eat the fruit, is rebelling against the just authority of God, rather than the unjust authority of a tyrant. God has given her the freedom to disobey Him, but in a perfect universe such a freedom cannot be exercised without damnation. Just as one has the freedom to end one's life whenever one chooses, but loses the freedom to enjoy the good things in life once one has done so, so Eve, when she has disrupted a perfect universe, cannot continue to enjoy its perfection. It may seem that her sin was small and the punishment great. This is true, if we assume the sin is literally the eating of the fruit. The act, however, represents the decision to disobey not some arbitrary authority, but the law and order that God has created out of Chaos so that man may live and enjoy life. The act of disobedience is dangerous because it threatens to bring about the destruction of the entire creative realm and the consequent return of Chaos. In conceiving and portraying the problem of obedience in this way, Milton is representing human action very realistically. If we do not live in accordance with the laws that make life possible and enjoyable for us, we are bound to suffer. For example, if we disobey the law of gravity we will be severely hurt or killed. If we disobey the laws governing effective international relations we will precipitate a war. And so on. It is important to understand that the disobedience of which Eve is guilty is an important kind, not a trivial one, and that her act is symbolic. Her character, then, appears vain and willful. She has adopted the cloak of reason, but the consequences of allowing pure reason to govern one's behavior without checking the assumptions on which the reasoning is based become quickly evident when we see what happens after the fruit is eaten. The result, in Eve's case, is that after she persuades Adam to join her in her disobedience, she must suffer banishment from Paradise, not only for herself and her husband, but for all her descendants as well.

THE SPEECH

In this speech Eve moves from the first tentative statement of possibility to the final certainly that will allow her to act as she desires to. We see the gradual increase of confidence as she persuades herself step by step that she is doing the right thing in disobeying the law of God.

Though she had previously recognized the importance of the fruit in an abstract way, she had not conceived any particular desire for it herself. The suggestions of the serpent have made it seem more desirable and less dangerous than she had thought, and she now looks at the fruit in a new way. The fact that the serpent has learned to speak on first eating the fruit proves to her the virtue of the fruit, despite the fact that it has been kept from man. It occurs to Eve for the first time that God may not be operating entirely in man's interests. If this is so, it would be advantageous to eat the fruit as quickly as possible.

God has Himself indicated the great value of the fruit by identifying it with the knowledge of good and evil. It does not occur to Eve that one can distinguish between good and evil only after one has done an evil thing and longs for the return of good. She thinks, rather, that the fruit conceals some good that has not yet been given her. Like a child who has been told that a thing is forbidden, Eve finds the forbidden thing more fascinating for that very reason and believes that it would not be forbidden if it did not have some value or give some pleasure. She further reasons that if she does not have the knowledge of good and evil, she cannot know good, and therefore does not possess the good—or if she does possess it, she does not recognize it. There is a certain amount of ironic truth in this statement. She will appreciate Paradise a great deal more after she has been ordered to leave it.

Eve in her own mind manipulates God into a logically untenable position. He is forbidding her knowledge, virtue, and wisdom. Such a prohibition cannot be good; therefore it should be broken. (Eve's argument here looks very much like Milton's own reason for serving a rebel government. The only difference is that Milton argued from assumptions he believed to be true; Eve, from assumptions she could have found false had she taken the time to examine them.)

Eve is caught in a momentary difficulty. She had obeyed God's command not only because she had never questioned its rightness, but also because she was afraid of the penalty of breaking it, which was death. Should she eat the fruit now and die, she might gain inner freedom from God's unjust law, but she would lose her outer freedom and not be able to use what she had gained. She escapes from the dilemma by observing that though the serpent has eaten (he actually has not, but she doesn't know this), he is not dead. Therefore, if she eats, she will not die. It does not occur to her, either, that death may not be immediate, that the punishment may merely be eventual death, or loss of the immortality that Adam and Eve had so long as they obeyed God's command.

Because the serpent has evidently been permitted to eat what is denied to man, Eve sees an inversion of the natural order. This makes her jealous: the serpent has indulged in certain privileges she had thought reserved for man, and she therefore desires to outdo him by acquiring yet greater privileges, presumably those reserved for God. Furthermore, the serpent seems to have the privilege of eating the fruit without penalty of death, and, what is more, seems not to be jealous of his right, but freely to offer it to man. Since the beast has obviously not suffered any ill effects, there is nothing to fear. Furthermore, he is an informant from whom one can suspect no harm. Ironically, she sees him, because of his apparent position in the natural order of things, as being "far from deceit or guile."

Eve's next logical step toward a position from which she can act is to state that she cannot fear consequences about which she can know nothing. Since God has denied her the knowledge of good and evil, she cannot know anything to fear. She cannot even know God (good) or death (evil). She has reasoned her way into a position that is justified in her own own mind by lack of knowledge. She has no further fear of consequences. Her last four lines are beautifully ironic: "Here grows the cure of all": her ignorance will certainly be cured by the experience of eating the fruit, though not in the way she thinks. The inviting qualities of the fruit are typical of temptation. They will indeed "feed" both body and mind: body, by making it susceptible to death; mind, by making it the wiser for a sad experience.

The art with which Milton in so few lines makes a character who is believably good become believably corrupt is magnificent. Most poetry and drama are built on some combination of reason and emotion, with the emphasis usually on the latter. This passage depends almost entirely on reason for its effect, the single emotion being the increasing desire that Eve feels to do what she has been told not to do. Yet because of the way in which he has shown a particular mind at work, because of what is at stake, and because of the intensity of the desire that leads Eve too easily to accept the assumptions on which her reasoning is based, Milton has created something both dramatic and human, that, far from being mere dry philosophy, presents a challenge to the finest actress.

EVE DECIDES TO EAT THE FRUIT OF THE TREE OF KNOWLEDGE

Eve stands C, looking a few inches above her head at the fruit, which hangs from the tree, located DRC. Her right hand is extended, palm up but slightly cupped, toward the tree. The serpent is LC, next to Eve.

    Great are thy virtues, doubtless, best of fruits,
        Though kept from man, and worthy to be admired,
    Whose taste, too long forborne,

Extending her left hand slightly in the direction of the serpent, she looks down at him. Her right hand remains in its initial position.

                              at first assay
    Gave elocution to the mute, and taught
    The tongue not made for speech thy praise;

The left hand extends upward almost as far as it will reach, and she follows it with her eyes, looking up toward God.

> Thy praise He also who forbids thy use,
> Conceals not from us,

Left hand lowered to about chest level. She looks again toward the tree.

> naming thee the tree
> Of knowledge, knowledge both of good

A slight tremor runs through her, and she thinks of the fearful possibilities behind this next word. She looks down at the ground with almost a premonition of her guilt.

> and evil;

Pulling her hands down to her sides, but keeping the palms forward and the arms energetic, she looks up defiantly toward God. Her voice takes on a slightly icy and defiant quality.

> Forbids us then to taste,

Takes a step toward the tree, again raising her right hand toward it. Her voice is much warmer, but it has behind it a guilty seductiveness, something of the sound of a child who knows he is doing the wrong thing and is trying to persuade someone older that it is right.

> But His forbidding
> Commends thee more, while it infers the good
> By thee communicated,

Lowering her hand slightly, she appears rather coy. She sounds as if she is trying to persuade the tree that it will be to its advantage to satisfy her wants. She is, in a way, flattering the tree.

> and our want:

Looks at the audience, both hands extended about equally. Her voice becomes slightly louder, and takes on a purely rational sound. She is trying to disguise from herself the fact that she is giving in to desire by persuading herself that she is simply thinking logically in a purely disinterested way.

> For good unknown sure is not had; or, had
> And yet unknown, is as not had at all.

Raises her head so that she is looking up toward God. There is a hint of anger in her voice.

> In plain, then, what forbids He but to know,
> Forbids us good, forbids us to be wise?

Takes a step toward the tree and reaches up, grasping the fruit. She would pluck it at this moment but for a second thought.

> Such prohibitions bind not.

Slowly lowers her hand. Speaks slowly, and with awe.

Eve Decides to Eat the Fruit of the Tree of Knowledge / 157

>>But if death
>Bind us with after-bands, what profits then
>Our inward freedom?

Looks at the fruit, but does not reach toward it.

>>In the day we eat
>Of this fair fruit,

Turns away, facing C, her hands clasped at her waist with anxiety.

>>our doom is, we shall die.

Her eye lights on the serpent. She feels the sudden relief that comes with realizing one's apprehensions are false. This amounts to a minor triumph over God. Her face lights up, but with a guilty, defensive light.

>How dies the serpent? he hath eaten and lives,

Gestures alternately with both hands, working her focus again toward the front.

>And knows, and speaks, and reasons, and discerns,

Looks toward God with a triumphant smile.

>Irrational till then.

She looks again toward the audience, her thoughts seeking confirmation from an impartial point of view. Her tone has a hint of righteous indignation. She feels keenly the unfairness of what she protests.

>>For us alone
>Was death invented? or to us denied
>This intellectual food, for beasts reserved?

Looks again toward the serpent.

>For beasts, it seems;

She goes down on her knees, symbolically placing herself on a level with the beast. She looks at it feeling that it is a friend. Her voice has the warmth of an injured person sharing an injury with someone sympathetic.

>>yet that one beast which first
>Hath tasted, envies not, but brings with joy
>The good befallen him, author unsuspect,
>Friendly to man, far from deceit or guile.

Rises. Emphasis on the "I".

>What fear I, then?

Turns toward the tree, assuming a coy mask of innocence.

>>rather, what know to fear
>Under the ignorance of good and evil,
>Of God and death, of law or penalty?

Kate Swet as Eve:
"What hinders then
 To reach, and feed at once both body and mind?"

A few steps toward the tree, reaching out again with the right hand toward the fruit. Her tone is of one praising the tree rather strongly in order to gain its sympathy for her act. Each phrase should be stronger than the last.

> Here grows the cure of all, this fruit divine,
> Fair to the eye, inviting to the taste,
> Of virtue to make wise:

She reaches up and plucks the fruit, with her right hand.

>   what hinders then
> To reach,

She holds the fruit before her face, ready to eat.

>   and feed at once both body and mind?

She bites from the fruit, chews and swallows. Then she looks at the audience. Superficially, her expression is happy, but behind the smile there is the anxiety of one who has had her way and flown in the face of everything she has always believed to be right.

VOCAL AND PHYSICAL CHARACTERIZATION

Paradise Lost is an unusual work in that it contains in very scarce quantity many of the things we normally associate with great poetry. There are few clearly drawn characters. There is little in the way of dramatic event, aside from the skillfully described war in Heaven. There is even little that is observed either in human behavior or in nature. Nevertheless the work, long as it is, is almost unflagging in the power of its poetry. Perhaps this results from the fact that Milton himself is so deeply concerned about the subject of his poem that the intensity of his conviction provides all the power we need.

The passage we have here is almost unique in the poem in that it shows a character undergoing very rapid and decisive change. Such brilliant characterization, in addition to the power of Milton's belief that informs the rest of the poem, offers the actress a double opportunity, and yet one that cannot be fully realized. Milton is unlike Shakespeare and other great dramatists in that he never completely submerges his own personality in that of the character he is creating. Behind the words of Eve one can almost hear Milton commenting on their fallacies. Indeed Milton's Eve seems rather improbable as a human being in a certain sense. Anyone capable of the naïve assumptions and reactions that Eve is guilty of would have difficulty reasoning with as much apparent logic as Eve is using. It is only the skilled logician like Milton who can imagine such a thought process.

Thus the Eve that we are to see represents something that is partly the Eve that we would expect and partly the author speaking through his character, verbalizing thoughts that she would not have had in quite the same way.

The voice we are to hear, then, is an intelligent voice, not the naïve, simple, pristine one we would expect from an Eve who speaks completely for herself. It is Milton's voice, parodying the reasoning process with a kind of sorrow that such distorted use of it is possible. It is also a female voice going through the change that Milton has designed for it. To project this striking change requires skilled vocal control.

The voice must do two things: it must first project a particular human being who remains throughout the speech consistently one person. It must also reflect the changing attitude taking place within that person. Therefore, the suggestions that follow will not be effective unless they are very subtly employed. Indeed, they should be so subtle that they will not be noticeable unless one is actually looking for them. The result will be to give the audience a feeling for what is happening without immediately revealing the sources from which that feeling stems. Technique to accomplish such a result is not easily achieved; it is the greatest and most difficult kind of artistry.

At the beginning of the passage, Eve is still almost innocent. She has been tempted, it is true, and guilty thoughts have passed through her mind, but she has not yet made that decision from which there is no return. She has not yet taken an action she would find it difficult to defend. As a completely innocent person she had a free and happy quality in her speech. She had never known anything she needed to hide. She had never had the slightest necessity to weigh her words before she spoke. Everything was said just as it came to mind. There was a childlike quality in her, and her voice had the joy and beauty of that of a child who is, for the moment, completely happy. As she continues to speak, Eve gradually becomes corrupt; that is, she says to herself things that she would desire to conceal from God so long as she continues to believe them. By the end she is a person who is doing something she tries to make herself believe is right, but feels deep down inside to be wrong, if only because it contradicts the assumptions about the universe according to which she had previously lived. This causes a slight guilty edge to creep into her voice, a hardening, a defensiveness.

To achieve the quality necessary for the beginning, the actress will need to pitch her voice relatively high and inflect it upward toward the ends of phrases. A light quality, achieved by placing the voice high in the head, so that it seems to resonate in the region of the eyes, will give it a childlike effect. Perhaps a slight breathiness to soften it will add even more to the innocence.

By the end of the scene, the vocal patterns will have changed slightly. There will be a downward turn at the end of the phrase, almost a note of defiance in the voice. Pitch will remain the same, but perhaps the area of resonance will have lowered in the head so that Eve sounds more mature. Where the vowels have previously been emphasized, the consonants will begin to take on more importance, and will be made to sound sharper, giving the whole voice more brittleness. The breathiness should disappear, and in its place a slight twang should be heard, almost a resentful quality.

One very important thing to consider in Milton is the phrasing. Milton wrote in long periods, that is, sentences of almost paragraph length in which the interplay between various grammatical constructions is very complex and very interesting in its own right. This passage is less complex than many, but note that the first full stop does not occur until line thirteen. The actress must sense the cumulative effect of words and phrases in a unit as long as this, and not allow the effect to become choppy. A great deal of breath control is needed to give such a sentence its full effect. This is why Eve must retain some of the quality of Milton himself. She cannot really sound like a child, for no child could make convincing a series of constructions so long and beautifully organized as these.

It will be very difficult to integrate all the above qualities without producing apparent discontinuities in the character. A speech such as this one may not only take a great deal of work, but also a considerable period of time in which to allow its many elements to fuse in the mind. It may be well to work on the speech for a while and then put it aside, allowing it to begin to fit itself together in one's unconscious before one tries to put it into final form. To that end, work on things carefully and consciously and then try to forget about them and do the speech just as you feel it.

Physically, this scene is necessarily quite static. Eve stands before a tree and contemplates its fruit. There is no action until the speech is over, when she plucks the fruit and eats it. The action is an action of the mind.

This is a character for whom the word "classic" has tremendous meaning. She is an abstraction, a reasoning process, rather than a full human being. Her beauty, too, is abstract and idealized. It is so great that it almost dissuades the serpent from his purpose. It is achieved partly by the way she holds herself. She has the elegance of a beautiful painting or statue.

It would be awkward to hold a single pose throughout the speech. The particular poses hardly matter, so long as they are beautiful, and perhaps reflect some of the changes in attitude that Eve undergoes. The best way to learn the physical quality radiated by Eve is to study carefully sculpture and painting from classical Greece and Rome and the Renaissance, which is a realistic representation of the female form not as it is, but as the artist believes it should be. Pay particular attention to the positions of the fingers, wrists, and elbows. Notice the way the arms are placed so that they balance perfectly with the stance of the body as a whole. Practice several poses with a mirror until you can associate the feeling in your arms and body with the appearance that you make in the mirror.

BELINDA BEMOANS THE LOSS OF A LOCK OF HER HAIR

(from *The Rape of the Lock* by Alexander Pope)

Forever cursed be this detested day,
Which snatched my best, my favorite curl away!
Happy! ah, ten times happy had I been,
If Hampton Court these eyes had never seen!
Yet am not I the first mistaken maid,
By love of courts to numerous ills betrayed.
Oh had I rather unadmired remained
In some lone isle, or distant northern land;
Where the gilt chariot never marks the way,
Where none learn Ombre, none e'er taste Bohea!
There kept my charms concealed from mortal eye,
Like roses, that in deserts bloom and die.
What moved my mind with youthful lords to roam?
Oh had I stayed, and said my prayers at home!
'Twas this the morning omens seemed to tell,
Thrice from my trembling hand the patch-box fell;
The tottering china shook without a wind;
Nay, Poll sat mute, and Shock was most unkind!
A Sylph, too, warned me of the threats of fate,
In mystic visions, now believed too late!
See the poor remnants of these slight hairs!
My hands shall rend what even thy rapine spares.
These, in two sable ringlets taught to break,
Once gave new beauties to the snowy neck;
The sister-lock now sits uncouth, alone,
And in its fellow's fate foresees its own;
Uncurled it hangs, the fatal shears demands,
And tempts, once more, thy sacrilegious hands.
Oh hadst thou, cruel! been content to seize
Hairs less in sight, or any hairs but these!

COMMENTARY

The Poem

"In matters of grave importance," wrote Oscar Wilde in *The Importance of Being Earnest,* "style, not sincerity, is the vital thing." Many people in the 18th and 19th centuries lived as though this statement were really true. That form of comedy called comedy of manners criticizes its characters almost solely on the basis of how well they behave socially.

Perhaps Alexander Pope (1688–1744) is the greatest of all poets on the subject of manners and social behavior. Early in his life he had decided that his ideal would be to write "what oft was thought, but ne'er so well expressed," in other words, not to seek new subject matter or philosophy but to perfect his writing in style and manner. In the expression of ideas, he sought to sum up the philosophy of the age; in the description of people, to portray its social character. His characters are people of style rather than of genuine emotion.

Nothing better demonstrates the 18th century concern for manners than Pope's mock-epic poem *The Rape of the Lock* and the actual incident on which it was based. A certain Arabella Fermor had had a lock of her hair cut off at a party that took place in 1711, by a man whose station in life was considerably in advance of his behavior. A minor scandal resulted from the event and Pope was persuaded by a friend of his to write a poem making fun of it in order to soothe the feelings of the offended parties.

Pope turned for inspiration to his great predecessor, Milton, and wrote a poem that parodied the style of *Paradise Lost* and other similar epics. Trivial events were described in heroic, earth-shaking terms. The title of the poem is an example of this, for it suggests violence and conflict on a grand scale, rather than an error of social graces. In the poem, Belinda, the heroine, who represents the offended Arabella, attends a party at Hampton Court, a royal residence, where she wins a game of ombre (a fashionable card game) against a young baron. In retaliation, during the refreshments that follow, the Baron snips off a lock of her hair. In the aftermath of this incident there is considerable expression of ill-feeling.

Pope has elaborated the central action with a detailed description of Belinda's preparations for the party, and with mock-heroic descriptions of the social behavior of the characters, of the card game, and of the verbal byplay that follows the cutting of the lock. In addition, he has peopled the atmosphere with sylphs who watch over and attempt to assist the various characters, much as do the Greek gods in Homer's epics, or the angels in *Paradise Lost*. Some idea of the mock-heroic character of the narrative can be obtained from reading the description of the cutting off of the lock itself:

> The peer now spreads the glittering forfex*
>   wide,
> T'enclose the lock; now joins it, to divide.
> Even then, before the fatal engine closed,
> A wretched Sylph too fondly interposed;
> Fate urged the shears, and cut the Sylph in
>   twain,
> (But airy substance soon unites again)
> The meeting points the sacred hair dissever
> From the fair head, forever and forever!

This is the humor of overstatement, and it is the key to how the whole poem must be interpreted.

The Character

Belinda is like a child with only one desire: to impress others with her beauty. When that desire is frustrated, there is no other source of happiness in life. Like a

---

* a pair of scissors.

child, she bursts out with a tremendous temper tantrum, and that is what we see in this speech.

But Belinda has many qualities of which she is unaware, but which should be made clear in her portrayal. She is despicable, because she lives according to a system of values that exalts what is trivial and degrades what is important. The fact that the loss of a lock of her hair is the most tragic thing that can happen to her means that all other conceivable fates are less tragic and therefore less important. She is delightful, because she radiates charm and superficial dignity. If she were not charming, she would never have provoked the Baron to behave as he did. If she were not dignified, it would never have occurred to him that such an action could be harmful to her. She is laughable, because her position is so extreme as to be funny, and Pope's choice of words in which to portray that position wittily underscores its unnaturalness. She is poignant, because she is fully enough characterized so that we can believe it is possible for a real person to feel as she feels, and even as we laugh we imagine and empathize with her plight. That is why it is so important for the actress to portray her seriously and not to appear to be laughing at her. She is brittle, because her entire existence is based on a set of social assumptions that are very limited in time and place, and because we cannot imagine that she might continue to exist outside of that very limited milieu. The dominant impression she conveys is of a mixture of purity, beauty and silvery brightness. Throughout the poem, descriptive passages elaborate these three impressions of her. As is always true in the finest comedy, the humor is heightened by increasing the seriousness and richness and in some sense attractiveness of the character. The humor is always on the very edge of becoming extremely serious. If we cannot see why, given her own assumptions, Belinda behaves as she does, she will appear merely ridiculous, and cease to be funny. Her honor is the source of her levity, and her levity the source of her honor. Therefore, the actress must care, and care as deeply as Belinda does, that she has been the victim of a social indignity.

The Speech

For a child or a primitive person, everything associated with an evil thing partakes of some of that thing's evil. Belinda does not see the incident of losing her lock of hair as an isolated one; every occurrence during the day has played its part in the unraveling of her terrible fate. On her own level, she has something in common with Lady Macbeth, who feels that all the powers of evil have conspired to bring Duncan to her house at the time when she is ready to murder him.

Belinda imagines that she would be extremely happy if she could somehow have avoided her misery. All of the gaiety and glitter of Hampton Court (a palace outside London built in the time of Henry VIII, and the scene of highly fashionable social occasions), have been poisoned for her by this one incident, and she wishes she had never seen the place.

She turns her grief into a rueful moral observation: such is the fate of maidens who allow themselves to be corrupted by court life. The ideal maiden would somehow shield herself from influences like those under which she has fallen. The totality with which Belinda rejects the splendor of a past that a moment before she so innocently enjoyed is particularly ironic, considering the fact that she could not possibly exist without all the things she is now rejecting.

Belinda now seems to become totally irrational. Obviously she prizes her beauty because it causes her to be admired. Now that she has lost some of her beauty, however, she claims that she would have been happier had she never been admired. (It was, after all, the Baron's admiration of her beauty that caused him to desire a lock of her hair.) The absurdity of this reaction points up the fact that a young lady so treated ought to be at least a little flattered by the attention she has received. It is Belinda's failure to realize this kind of thing in addition to her melodramatic reaction to the situation that makes her absurd.

She develops the idea of her exile from society by mentioning some of its beauties: the gilt chariot, the card game, bohea (a superior kind of black tea). The image of roses blooming and dying in the desert is almost touching, although we quickly reflect that roses are unlikely to grow anywhere outside of rose gardens, and Belinda's charms would also be unlikely to survive under the conditions she is now describing.

Belinda next begins to think that in some way she is perhaps responsible for her fate. Perhaps she should have stayed at home, away from the "youthful lords," and said her prayers. She should at least have paid attention to the omens, which (as they do in Greek epics) ought to have warned her against what was coming. Three times (three is a mystical, foreboding number) the patch-box (containing "patches" or little cloth beauty spots which could be fixed to the face) fell from her hand. Her china, probably displayed on a plate rail, trembled and for no apparent reason threatened to fall. Poll (her parrot) had nothing to say to her that morning, and Shock (her lap-dog) was not his usual friendly self. While she slept, she had had a dream brought to her by her protecting Sylphs, that should have warned her of the dangers to follow. (This detail is a reference to a scene in *Paradise Lost* in which Eve is made to dream of evil things under the influence of Satan, and the dream foreshadows the terrible disobedience of which she will later be guilty.)

At long last, Belinda becomes specific about her situation. She grasps in her hands the hair that has been shortened and looks mournfully at it. In a frenzy she determines to cut it off further and recalls the beauty it once had. The poor "sister lock" now appears strange and alone, no longer balanced by its partner. Though both locks had been carefully curled, the remaining one is now uncurled, perhaps out of sympathy for its lost mate, and demands to be cut off too.

Now Belinda employs a tactic guaranteed to shame the light-hearted Baron. She turns to him and tearfully suggests that he may be tempted to cut off the remaining lock. She then says that the hairs he has cut are the hairs she could least bear to part with.

We have looked at Belinda's emotions as if they were to be taken seriously, and in the process completely lost sight of the humor. The actress must begin by looking at them in just such a way. But once Belinda is clear to her, and she is capable of sympathizing with her plight, she must remember that she must also make the audience laugh. Just the right amount of exaggeration of a sincerely felt emotion will do this effectively, whereas attempting to mimic the emotions without really feeling them will produce an effect that is dull and lifeless if it is not grotesque and tasteless.

Some of the genius of this passage lies in its attempt to make us take it seriously. We laugh at the absurdity of Belinda's ranting during the early part of her speech, but as we look at her contemplating the actual loss of part of her hair, as we see her tearfully and helplessly turn to the wretch who has desecrated her, we are not quite sure where we stand anymore. This forces the laughter back on ourselves, for certainly we all have some of Belinda's vanity in us, and her exaggerated melodrama is an extension of a universal human failing. Pope has here successfully parodied a major literary form, satirized a segment of his own society, and commented tellingly on human nature. Any one of these achievements by itself would have been enough. The combination of them has produced a masterpiece.

BELINDA BEMOANS THE LOSS OF A LOCK OF HER HAIR

Belinda stands LC, behind the card table at which she was sitting when the lock was cut from her hair. C is Thalestris, Belinda's friend, who has just asked Sir Plume to try to retrieve the lock from the Baron. Sir Plume stands RC. He and Thalestris regard the Baron who, DR, has just refused to return the lock. Belinda is "half drowned in tears;/On her heaved bosom [hangs] her drooping head,/Which, with a sigh she [raises]." She wrings her hands and looks tragically toward the ceiling.

  Forever cursed be this detested day,
  Which snatched my best, my favorite curl away!

Hands out to sides, chest level.

  Happy,

Enraged, she roles her hands into fists and gnashes her teeth.

  ah, ten times happy had I been,[1]

Looks quickly about her on all sides, blaming Hampton Court itself for what has happened.

  If Hampton Court

Clutching her hands at her waist again, she again looks down.

    these eyes had never seen!

Crosses DL, breathing heavily, showing her anger by turning her back on all those present. There is in her voice a hint of the attitude, "I knew it all the time; I should have expected nothing more!"

  Yet am not I the first

"Mistaken" is very pointed, very self-pitying.

    mistaken maid,
  By love of courts to numerous ills betrayed.

Sits in a chair DL, her left hand to her forehead, her chin up, in a tragic pose.

  Oh had I rather unadmired remained
  In some lone isle, or distant northern land;

Again wringing her hands.

  Where the gilt chariot never marks the way,

A ferocious glance at the card table.

> Where none learn Ombre,

Casts her eyes toward the floor on her left. Her voice is low and very tragic, slowing down in pace.

> none e'er taste Bohea!* ²*

Tries to force herself to be calm, to assume daintiness. Sits up straight, her hands in her lap. Looks very beautiful.

> There kept my charms concealed from mortal eye,
> Like roses, that in deserts bloom and die.

Head bent a little, shoulders up, looking down toward the left, hands in same position. Voice heavy and liquid.

> What moved my mind with youthful lords to roam?

Hands covering eyes in position of weeping, but not weeping. Weariness in the voice.

> Oh had I stayed, and said my prayers at home!

As if making a new discovery, she stands and looks forward contemplatively. Her hands are relaxed at her sides. Emphasis on "this".

> 'Twas this the morning omens seemed to tell,

Right hand up in position of holding patch-box. She looks at it, recalling the action she is describing. A slight tremor in her voice.

> Thrice from my trembling hand the patch-box fell;

She looks up and toward the right, at about the level of a plate rail.

> The tottering china shook without a wind;³

Increasingly the almost mystical character of what has happened impresses her. Her voice takes on an awed quality. She looks toward positions that might have been held by Poll and Shock.

> Nay, Poll sat mute, and Shock was most unkind!

Her voice becomes more ecstatic. She looks ahead and takes a step forward, right hand up above head level.

> A Sylph, too, warned me of the threats of fate,
> In mystic visions, now believed too late!

Wheeling suddenly to the right, she crosses to DC. Her right hand reaches up across her body to the left side of her face, where the lock has been cut off. She speaks ferociously to the Baron.

> See the poor remnants of these slight hairs!

With both hands, she grasps the lock on the right side of her head, and looks for a moment as if she will pull it off. The ferocity increases almost to a growl.

Donna Anderson as Belinda: "Forever cursed be this detested day."

My hands shall rend what even thy rapine spares.

Suddenly, she is pathetic. She almost caresses with her right hand the poor remnants on her left. There is a sob in her voice.

These in two sable ringlets taught to break,
Once gave new beauties to the snowy neck;

Looks toward the audience, turning her body out slightly. Her tragic gaze serves to identify her own fate with that of the sister-lock. Aside from a slight tremor, her tone is distant, almost cold.

The sister-lock now sits uncouth, alone,
And in its fellow's fate foresees its own;

Tears come to her eyes, but she maintains her stance.

Uncurled it hangs, the fatal shears demands,
And tempts, once more, thy sacrilegious hands.

Turns again to the Baron, her voice on a swelling tidal wave of grief and ferocity until the end, when she is right on the verge of screaming. Her right hand extends the remnant hairs as far toward the Baron as they will go.

Oh hadst thou, cruel! been content to seize
Hairs less in sight, or any hairs but these!

NOTES

[1] rhymes with "seen."
[2] rhymes with "way."
[3] rhymes with "kind."

VOCAL AND PHYSICAL CHARACTERIZATION

Inasmuch as *The Rape of the Lock* closely resembles in its style many of the popular plays of its day, some idea of the conditions of the theatre of the time will help us to understand how Belinda might best be acted.

Going to the theatre in the 18th century was very fashionable, although still considered just a shade immoral. Frequently one went there as much to meet one's friends as to see the play. Audiences talked throughout most of the performances, and were very demonstrative in expressing their feelings about whatever parts of the play they paid any attention to. The only actors who could survive such treatment were those who would be considered by our standards extremely artificial in the emotional intensity of their style. Acting had more in common with trying to fascinate an angry mob than it did with entertaining the passive audiences we find today. Every moment he was onstage, the actor had to try to enthrall the audience either by the sensational nature of his acting, or by its humor, or by both. The plays tended to be either very funny, or extremely melodramatic, or (as in the present case) both; but they were always highly stylized. That is, the way actors walked and the way they talked were far more important to the audience than any real emotion they might feel. In fact, actors developed particular poses that they associated with particular emotions: there was almost a vocabulary of gestures.

The actress who performs Belinda, if she is true to the spirit of the 18th century, will render the character both stylized and superficial. She should not herself laugh at what is happening; but she should enable the audience to laugh both at the absurdity of Belinda's excessive emotions, and at the style of the acting itself. Perhaps she can work out an elaborate series of gestures into which she falls easily, almost automatically, so that they seem at the same time graceful and absurd. Bear in mind, though, that we are talking only about the externals of the performance, not contradicting what has been said previously about interpretation.

Belinda will instinctively do everything possible to accentuate her beauty. Even in the supreme moment of grief her sense of her own elegance will never leave her. Some of the comedy results from this character trait. Her gestures should be extreme, but always elegant. They should also be relevant to what she is saying. There should be no excessive primping. The desire to appear to go to the extremes of passion and yet control every gesture by giving it just the right stylistic touch will give her behavior an incongruity that reinforces Pope's satirical point.

Belinda is accustomed to wearing very long, very full dresses, with crinolines and petticoats. Being a member of the upper class and frequently appearing in society, she must wear these things a great deal of the time and look natural in them. Whenever she goes upstairs or down, she must lift her dress slightly so that she will not trip on it. Sitting down requires careful arrangement of her dress so that it will not be crumpled too badly, or look unattractive. She cannot stand very close to anything because of the expanse of her dress, and consequently must be aware of her surroundings at all times. Her social standing also requires that she have very good posture and excellent coordination. Her long experience with these things has made Belinda do them naturally. When she walks downstairs, for example, her hand lifting her skirts works automatically and is perfectly coordinated with the action of her legs, so that she does not have to look down. The effect of all this is that Belinda is always conscious of how she looks, and never makes a single movement or gesture that does not add something of value to the impression she is trying to create.

The actress should strive for a voice that will emphasize Belinda's femininity and helplessness and yet, through its precision, will show her indomitable *savoir-faire*. The voice should be heavily inflected to suggest the superficial quality of a personality that places undue emphasis on the importance of the social graces. It should also shift rather abruptly from melodramatic self-pity ("Uncurled it hangs . . .") to aggressive contempt ("Oh hadst thou, cruel! . . .").

AASE SEARCHES FOR HER SON

(from *Peer Gynt* by Henrik Ibsen)

SCENE—By a mountain lake, on boggy moorland. A storm is blowing up. Aase, in despair, is calling and searching in every direction. Solveig can scarcely keep pace with her. Her parents and Helga are a little way behind. Aase beats the air with her arms and tears her hair.

Everything's against me with the might of anger! The skies and the water and the hateful mountains! Fogs from the skies are rolling to mislead him—treacherous waters will delude and drown him—mountains will crush or slip away beneath him—! And all these people! They are out to kill him! By God, they shall not! I can't do without him! The oaf! To think the devil thus should tempt him! (*Turns to Solveig.*) Ah, my girl, one simply can't believe it. He, who was always full of lies and nonsense—he, who was only clever with his talking—he, who had never done a thing worth telling—he—! Oh, I want to laugh and cry together! We were such friends in our needs and troubles. For, you must know, my husband was a drunkard, made us a byword in the neighbors' gossip, brought all our good estate to rack and ruin, while I and Peerkin sat at home together—tried to forget—we knew no better counsel; I was too weak to stand up stoutly to it. It is so hard to face the fate that's coming; and so one tries to shake one's sorrows off one, or do one's best to rid one's mind of thinking. Some fly to brandy, others try romancing; so we found comfort in the fairy stories all about trolls and princes and such cattle—tales, too, of stolen brides—but who would ever think that such stories in his mind would linger? (*Becomes terrified again.*) Ah, what a screech! A nixie or a kelpie! Peer! Oh, my Peer!—Up there upon the hillock—! (*Runs up onto a little hillock and looks over the lake. Solveig's parents come up to her.*) Not a thing to be seen!

COMMENTARY

THE PLAY

Peer Gynt was originally intended as a poem, not a play, although Ibsen produced it as a play shortly after he wrote it. It is too long for an evening's entertainment, contains many actions difficult to represent on the stage, and is even more rambling in its effect than most plays of the romantic period, many of which tended to get as far away as possible from the classical unities of time, place, and action. Nevertheless, it is an exciting and beautiful and lovable play, a play to which one returns again and again with renewed interest.

The action of the play covers the first half of the 19th century, and is set in Norway and in Africa. Almost the only source of unity is the character of Peer himself, whose adventures are followed from his early manhood to a time when he is very close to death. Ibsen is particularly interested in the relationship between Peer and the women in his life: Aase (pronounced aw-suh), his nagging mother; the faithful Solveig; the troll princess who seduces him; and the beautiful Anitra, who takes all his money and runs away. Perhaps the most important of these is Aase, who dominates the first half of the play. Nearly all of Peer's character traits can be traced to his relationship with her. At the end of his life, though he has pursued relentlessly the development of what he calls "the Gyntian self," he has failed to develop a character either sufficiently good or sufficiently bad to be worthy of Heaven or Hell. In one of the fantasy scenes of the play, he is met by a Button Moulder, who tells him he will have to be melted down and used as material for making other people. His last efforts are attempts to avoid this fate. Why is Peer, despite a great many varied activities, neither a man of virtue nor a great sinner? We can find the answer in the character of his mother.

The Character

Aase is a woman who has not borne up very well under a hard life. Her husband was a drunkard, and she tries to compensate for her disappointment in him by centering all her interest in her son. In order to escape her misery she would tell him fairy stories, and as he grew older he too began to take refuge in such flights from reality. He found that in addition to flattering his own ego he could deeply affect her by telling her fantastic stories about his own escapades, which she never quite knew whether to believe or not.

Aase's greatest difficulty is that she really does not want her son to grow up, and when he does she becomes terribly fearful of being left alone. She reacts to this in two ways: by treating her son as if he were a child, and by dwelling more and more on her memories of what a wonderful child he was. She so exaggerated her expectations of him that he constantly disappointed them; and so, in addition to seeing him as a wonderful child she constantly worried about his bad qualities. She is inconsistent, temperamental, cantankerous, and bitter about all the happiness she has missed. She has isolated herself from the rest of the world, sharing her life almost exclusively with her son. Consequently, an attack on her son is an attack on her; and she can never have a moment's rest when he is in any way failing her expectations. In order to preserve her image of him, she has come to explain his bad qualities as the result of temptations by the devil.

The Scene

While attending a wedding party, Peer has stolen the bride away and taken her off to the mountains with him. Just before doing so, he has met Solveig, who has fallen deeply in love with him. Solveig and her parents set out with Aase to seek the runaway Peer. In her despair at not being able to find him, Aase begins to reminisce.

Aase interprets the difficulties that arise during her search for Peer as a personal attack on her by Nature. She feels that everything is conspiring to make her miserable and destroy her son. She cannot accept the fact that Peer is responsible for what he has done and should be punished for it. She believes that because he is her son he should be sacred, and she becomes angry at the people who with the bride's father are trying to find him and punish him.

Because she needs him so much, and because he has disappointed and deserted her, Aase becomes angriest of all at Peer. But she protects Peer from losing her love by assuming that it is the devil's fault that he has behaved as he has.

Sharing her sorrow with Solveig, she indulges in a mother's loving reminiscence about the boy whom she does not believe can or should grow up and leave her. At the same time, she cannot conceal a little pride that Peer, who always seemed such a simple child, should finally have done something really impressive, even if it is evil. Perhaps she is actually glad that Peer has gotten back at the neighbors for all their ugly gossiping.

The despair she feels, now that Peer is gone and she cannot find him, makes all the misery of her past flood over her, and she must share with someone the feelings of weakness and helplessness she has had all those years. Now that she has expressed her anger and despair against everyone else, she begins to feel a little guilty: perhaps it was the tales she and her son told each other that put into Peer's mind the idea of stealing a bride. Her mood is broken by a screech from some bird or animal that sounds to her like one of the mythical creatures that are supposed to live in the wilds. Recovering from her instinctive fear, she realizes that it may have been stirred by Peer's movement in the distance—her hope is suddenly renewed. But after she has searched the countryside with her eyes, the hope is lost again.

The desires and fears that fill the life of a poor woman who has lived most of her life alone with her son have seldom been more beautifully captured than in this scene, in which the immediate action brings to life memories and feelings that span a lifetime. The ability to capture in a few short lines the essence of a character's whole past life is among the things that make Ibsen one of the greatest of all playwrights.

AASE SEARCHES FOR HER SON

Aase enters UR and runs to DL. Solveig enters behind her, and stands at UR. As Aase runs across the stage, we can see that she is quite old, and that she is physically exhausted. At the same time, she runs quite rapidly, with desperation, looking wildly about her as she goes, and with her hands up in front of her to help her keep her balance and protect her in case she should fall. When she reaches DL, she sees the mountain lake, which forces her to stop. Realizing that she cannot continue running, she suddenly feels with full force the hopelessness of her situation. The energy drains from her. Her shoulders fall forward. She suddenly looks much older. The energy that has been used for physical purposes suddenly seeks an outlet in her emotions. She begins to weep convulsively.

The actress may wish to precede her entrance with several cries of "Peer!" and to continue these as she rushes across the stage, climaxing them with one last desperate cry as she comes upon the lake.

Everything's against me with the might of anger!

Keeping her shoulders slumped, she looks up at the sky, then down at the water, then wheels around, with her back to the audience, looking up at the mountains behind her.

The skies and the water and the hateful mountains!

She turns again to the front, and her left hand sweeps upward in a curving motion, taking in the expanse of the skies.

    Fogs from the skies are rolling to mislead him—

Both hands reach outward and downward, toward the lake.

    treacherous waters will delude and drown him—

With a sweeping motion she turns her back to the audience and gestures up toward the mountains, about to deliver the next line. Then the full force of what she is about to say hits her and elicits a sharp intake of breath through the teeth. She clasps her hands at her waist and moves toward the center of the stage slowly and with her head down, speaking softly but intensely.

    mountains will crush or slip away beneath him—!

She stands still, with her eyes closed. The terrible injustice of the way the whole world seems united against her son hits her with terrible violence and she lashes out against it. The line starts softly, but explodes on the word "people," on which her head is thrown back and her clenched teeth are shown. At the same moment, her arms are pulled down to her sides, and her fists clenched.

    And all these people!

She realizes that her son may really be killed by his pursuers. She has never thought of that possibility before, and she is terrified. Her voice sounds soft and helpless. Her hands go limp.

    They are out to kill him!

She cries out in anguish, feeling that because she does not want Peer to be killed he cannot be killed. Her anguish makes her feel powerful enough to prevent such an action all by herself. Again there is tension in her body, showing that she is ready to fight. Her hands are raised clenched to the level of her chest. Her face is contorted.

    By God, they shall not! I can't do without him!

She becomes resentful of Peer for creating the situation in which she now finds herself. She brings her fists down to waist level, as if pounding an imaginary surface.

    The oaf!

Shakes her head ruefully.

    To think the devil thus should tempt him!

Solveig has crossed from UR to RC and now stands to the right of Aase. Aase turns to her, and puts her arm around her, drawing strength and sympathy from her knowledge that Solveig loves Peer.

    Ah, my girl, one simply can't believe it.

Florence Johnson as Aase: "Peer! Oh, my Peer!—"

Together they sit on a rock, C. Aase looks off dreamily into the distance, recalling Peer's childhood. She now seems very relaxed and still. Her dreams make her feel, and even appear, much younger.

> He, who was always full of lies and nonsense—

A smile crosses her face as she thinks of some clever nonsense that particularly delighted her, while at the same time she doesn't lose sight of the fact that Peer never accomplished anything.

> he, who was only clever with his talking—

The smile is gone. There is regret for her disappointed hopes for Peer, but she feels guilty for the regret because she needs to love him.

> he, who had never done a thing worth telling—

She reminds herself of what Peer has just done. He seems strange to her—this is not the Peer she had always known. She shakes her head in disbelief.

> he—!

Looks at Solveig, shaking her head and smiling sadly.

> Oh, I want to laugh and cry together! We were such friends in
> our needs and troubles.

Looks down at her hands lying in her lap and studies them carefully. It embarrasses her to tell Solveig the family secrets, but she feels a tremendous need for the relief that will come from telling them. Besides, she feels that Peer must already have told Solveig these things.

> For, you must know, my husband was a drunkard, made us a byword
> in the neighbors' gossip, brought all our good estate to rack and ruin,
> while I and Peerkin sat at home together—

Shakes her head. The burden of the memory is very heavy. Her voice reflects the heaviness.

> tried to forget—

She looks straight ahead, biting her lip, tears just about to come, feeling the terrible injustice of her fate, feeling her own innocence, and how little she has deserved all that she has had to endure.

> we knew no better counsel; I was too weak to stand up stoutly to it.

Looks at Solveig for a moment, feeling her youth and innocence, and consequently how little she can understand of what suffering really is. Then pats her gently on the shoulder, rises, and crosses DL, slowly.

> It is so hard to face the fate that's coming; and so one tries to shake
> one's sorrows off one, or do one's best to rid one's mind

Sob on the word "thinking."

> of thinking.

Choking back her tears, she raises her chin higher and looks off into the distance, making the whole thing abstract in her mind.

  Some fly to brandy, others try romancing;

Her voice becomes warmer. These are the happiest moments of her life that she is recalling.

  so we found comfort in the fairy stories all about trolls and princes and such cattle—

Aase is one who cannot enjoy a moment's happiness without feeling guilty for doing so. She recalls a tale that might have put into Peer's head the idea for what he has done. Her face is contorted, she again gnaws her lip, and her hands clutch at one another. Her voice is flat and expressionless.

  tales, too, of stolen brides—

She feels as if she has been accused, and hastens to proclaim her innocence. She turns toward Solveig, and there is painful pleading in her voice.

  but who would ever think that such stories in his mind would linger?

Is it because she can no longer live with these painful thoughts that she suddenly notices sounds that had gone unnoticed before, or is there a sudden cry for the first time? In any case, she runs terrified toward DR, her hands up, self-protectingly, glancing back over her shoulder in the direction from which the sound has come.

  Ah, what a screech! A nixie or a kelpie!

Looking now out in the direction of DL, she thinks she sees a movement in the distance. It must be Peer! She cries out at the top of her lungs, hoping he can hear her.

  Peer! Oh, my Peer!—

She tells herself that she can see him better from a high place L, looking over the lake. She rushes to it and scrambles up on it, clutching her skirts.

  Up there upon the hillock—!

She stands for a long moment, peering into the distance. The movement she previously saw is not repeated. She clutches her hands, desperately hoping, but as we watch, the hope drains out of her, and the clutching becomes a wringing of the hands, the eyes blink tears, the mouth is tight to hold back the sobs. She senses that Solveig's parents have come up beside her, and she looks down at them, shaking her head sadly.

  Not a thing to be seen!

VOCAL AND PHYSICAL CHARACTERIZATION

  Aase is a poor woman who has led a very difficult life. Though she may be as young as her late thirties, she looks and acts a great deal older. In addition, the long search for Peer and her deep grief and anxiety have exhausted her, intensifying the effect of age even further.

The thing that is most difficult for a young person to realize is the weariness and physical heaviness that accompany age. One who enjoys physical activity, and who experiences no effort in most everyday actions, cannot imagine easily what it is like to have to make an effort to do even the slightest thing. An old person is used to making such efforts. Aase is not conscious at every moment that it is an effort that she is making, because she has gotten used to her physical condition; but because every moment is difficult, she is short of breath and given to considerable economy of movement.

To get the physical feeling associated with age, lift some heavy object, or press your hands tightly together, pushing them against each other from opposite directions. The resistance you are meeting is the resistance that an old person feels within each of his muscles. To get the effect of age, you will have to create this artificially throughout your body. Don't make a single motion without holding back on it inside the muscle, so that the motion is slower and more calculated than usual, and perhaps trembles ever so slightly under the strain.

The same kind of tension should affect the voice. The sounds do not come easily, and they are difficult to control. Because of this, phrases will be shorter than would be otherwise natural, and some words may be repeated as a result of faltering. Be careful not to strain your voice by tensing up your throat. Rather, give the sound a nasal quality and let it tremble a little. Remember, too, that Aase is still full of vitality, and her age should be rather hinted at than fully stated. Her constant struggle with the limitations you have artificially created has made Aase accustomed to them, and she handles them more easily and comfortably than you will at first. It will take practice to make your aging effect seem natural.

Because Aase is emotionally unstable, there will have to be a spontaneity, almost a wildness, in her behavior that contrasts with the quality suggested above. Though her gestures are held back by the difficulty of making them, they are not studied. When Aase feels an emotion, she responds to it immediately and without the slightest restraint. Reacting to the shriek, she jumps up just as rapidly as her old body will allow her to. There is a good deal of huffing and puffing, sighing, whining, weeping, and spontaneous joy in Aase's speech. It will be difficult to capture all of her different kinds of excitability without seeming to shift characters altogether, but you must give Aase a wide range of emotion and at the same time consistency of personality.

ON BEING TOO FREQUENTLY PROPOSED TO

(from *An Ideal Husband* by Oscar Wilde)

Well, Tommy has proposed to me again. Tommy really does nothing but propose to me. He proposed to me last night in the music-room, when I was quite unprotected, as there was an elaborate trio going on. I didn't dare to make the smallest repartee, I need hardly tell you. If I had, it would have stopped the music at once. Musical people are so absurdly unreasonable. They always want one to be perfectly dumb at the very moment when one is longing to be absolutely deaf. Then he proposed to me in broad daylight this morning in front of that dreadful statue of Achilles. Really, the things that go on in front of that work of art are quite appalling. The police should interfere. At luncheon I saw by the glare in his eye that he was going to propose again, and I managed to check him in time by assuring him that I was a bimetallist. Fortunately I don't know what bimetallism means. And I don't believe anybody else does either. But the observation crushed Tommy for ten minutes. He looked quite shocked. And then Tommy is so annoying in the way he proposes. If he proposed at the top of his voice, I should not mind so much. That might produce some effect on the public. But he does it in a horrid confidential way. When Tommy wants to be romantic he talks to one just like a doctor. I am very fond of Tommy, but his methods of proposing are quite out of date. I wish, Gertrude, you would speak to him, and tell him that once a week is quite often enough to propose to anyone, and that it should always be done in a manner that attracts some attention.

COMMENTARY

THE PLAY

Oscar Wilde wrote *An Ideal Husband* in 1895, setting it in the fashionable London of his own day. Bernard Shaw, then a drama critic, summed up Wilde's gifts by writing, "In a certain sense Mr. Wilde is to me our only thorough playwright. He plays with everything: with wit, with philosophy, with drama, with actors and audience, with the whole theatre." This remark should be taken to heart by the actor. Wilde's plays are games in which the trivial is made serious, and the serious trivial.

An Ideal Husband is a curious mixture of comedy of manners and problem play. That is, some of the characters are involved in situations that make fun of the way people behave in society, whereas others are involved in a plot of intrigue in which an English statesman must decide between sacrificing his whole career and upholding a position he believes to be right. The play raises the question of the conflict between a man's loyalty to his family and his career, and his loyalty to society. It also raises the question of the proper attitude toward love in marriage. Should husband and wife expect perfection of each other, or can they still love each other once they have discovered mutual imperfections? These questions have been dealt with far more effectively by more serious playwrights, most notably Ibsen. It is the lighter moments, those characterized by the observation quoted above from Shaw, in which Wilde is at his best, and the scene we have here is such a moment.

No one has more brilliantly captured the absurdity of the upper class Victorian in all his glittering inanity than Wilde. The thing in which he is distinguished above all other playwrights is his gift for the ironic epigram. His best play, *The Importance of Being Earnest,* is filled with statements that wreak havoc with Victorian assumptions about life, such as, "If the lower orders don't set us a good example, what on earth is the use of them?" "Divorces are made in Heaven." "Relations are simply a tedious pack of people who haven't got the remotest knowledge of how to live, nor the smallest instinct about when to die." The secret of this kind of wit is the selection of some subject about which most people have sentimental feelings that amount to a cliché, and the inversion of some part of the feeling in order to produce the laughter of surprise. It is important that the inversion not be so violent as to produce disgust, but rather make us suddenly aware that our normal behavior often conflicts with our assumptions about what it should be. Thus, we assume that the higher classes ought to set the example, that marriages are made in heaven, and that one should love and seek out the company of one's relations, but we often behave as if these assumptions were not true.

The selection we have is a beautiful example of an extended ironic epigram. The assumption that a proposal of marriage ought to be made seriously and only once, is here inverted, and such a proposal is described in detail as a rather boring waste of time that is frequently, even mechanically, repeated. Elsewhere in the play Mabel says, "It is one of Tommy's days for proposing. He always proposes on Tuesdays and Thursdays, during the Season."

THE CHARACTER

Mabel Chiltern is a comparatively minor character in *An Ideal Husband,* and is one of those who are primarily caricatures. Wilde describes her as follows:

[She] is a perfect example of the English type of prettiness, the apple-blossom type. She has all the fragrance and freedom of a flower. There is ripple after ripple of sunlight in her hair, and the little mouth, with its parted lips, is expectant, like the mouth of a child. She has the fascinating tyranny of youth, and the astonishing courage of innocence. To sane people she is not reminiscent of any work of art. But she is really like a Tanagra statuette, and would be rather annoyed if she were told so.

The key to Mabel's character is the Tanagra statuette. She has that combination of rich beauty and almost rough simplicity that characterizes these early Greek works, which have not yet achieved the sophistication of the later sculpture more usually associated with Greece. She should sparkle with innocence. Her childlike quality should be almost overbearing. To say that she possesses the tyranny of youth means that she demands as her right things that older people assume will be difficult to acquire. These include both the attention that her beauty naturally draws and agreement with her point of view, which she assumes is necessarily correct. To say that she has the courage of innocence means that because she has led a sheltered life and has never experienced evil, she is not afraid to do and say things that older people would be more timid about. To say that she is not reminiscent of any work of art means that she has the purity and freshness of nature; in the context of her own society, there is nothing studied in her behavior; but by the standards of modern American culture her behavior would seem very carefully studied, as we shall further point out when discussing her vocal and physical characterization.

The contrast between the simplicity and childlikeness of Mabel's behavior and the cynicism of her words is one of the major sources of humor. Poor Tommy is completely blind to the cynicism, but continues to propose without any knowledge of the state of her mind. He appears ridiculously fervent and inept in Mabel's characterization of him.

Mabel is a direct descendant of Belinda in Pope's *The Rape of the Lock*. What Belinda has devoted her life to achieving, Mabel has acquired almost effortlessly: beauty, social grace, perfect charm. But both young ladies have many of the same concerns in life, and many of the same attitudes about it. Both make much of trivial matters and little of important ones. Mabel is more whimsical in her outlook; it is doubtful whether she could get as melodramatic about anything as Belinda does. In general, however, she is Belinda with less stiffness and a good, though somewhat perverse, sense of humor.

The Scene

The scene is the morning-room at the home of the principal character, Sir Robert Chiltern. Mabel Chiltern has come into the room "in the most ravishing frock" to find her sister-in-law, Lady Gertrude Chiltern, in conversation with one Lord Goring. Mabel makes an engagement with Lord Goring to go riding the next morning, and promises not to bring Tommy Trafford, who she says is in great disgrace. After Lord Goring leaves, Mabel asks Lady Chiltern to speak to Tommy about his dreadful habit of proposing.

Tommy is a secretary to Mabel's brother, an important British statesman. We imagine Tommy, a man of the utmost seriousness and sense of his own importance, surreptitiously seeking opportunities to propose to Mabel. We imagine him going through the motions with the greatest concern about the proper manner in which to propose and with very little awareness of how Mabel is actually reacting to him. Proposing makes this stuffy, unromantic man completely ridiculous. We laugh at him the more readily because we never see him in the play—he is created entirely in our imagination.

Mabel's concern is not that of a young lady who is sorry to hurt a lover's feelings, but rather that of a person aware only of the event itself, or rather of the style in which it occurs. Tommy having proposed to her in the music-room while a trio was being played, Mabel could say nothing. Had she answered him, the musicians, irritated by her desire to talk, would have stopped playing, and her reply would have been heard by everyone. This leads Mabel to observe that musical people are unreasonable enough to demand that others listen when they play.

The statue of Achilles to which Mabel refers is close to the Hyde Park Speakers' Corner, where anyone who wishes to speak publicly on behalf of some cause may do so. It is therefore, in a sense, one of the most public places one can find in all London, and the most inappropriate place possible for a scene of intimacy. Notice that Mabel, in her snobbish way, does not distinguish between Tommy's proposal to her and the other things that happen "in front of that work of art." It is all beneath her.

About ten years before *An Ideal Husband*

was written, England had undergone a depression in trade, had had the matter studied, and had been unable to conclude whether she should follow the existing practice of basing the value of money on the value of gold, or institute a new practice of using both gold and silver as standards. Those who held the latter view were called bimetallists, and many of them were quite vocal politically, though their views were never accepted by the government. The people with whom Mabel is associated in the play are actively concerned about economic policies, and it is probable that for Tommy the term "bimetallist" had a great deal of significance. Mabel says that she doesn't know what "bimetallism" means, which is a commentary on her ignorance of all issues aside from matters of etiquette. She goes on to say that no one else does either, indicating that she has probably heard a great deal of inconclusive discussion of the implications of bimetallism among her associates (though there is none in the play). The humor of the situation stems again from incongruity: Tommy, who is concerned with matters of the heart, is suddenly stymied by an economic reference that leaves him at a loss for words. Mabel is hardly the sort of person he would expect to take any position on economics at all!

Mabel's desire that Tommy speak "at the top of his voice" shows that she is interested in Tommy's proposals only because they are likely to attract attention to her desirability. She is satisfied with proposals once a week that take place publicly, because they will be just sufficient to prove to her, and to others, that she is an attractive girl. She doesn't like to have Tommy talk to her in a low, intimate voice, because the only people who have ever done that to her have been doctors, and what they have had to say has always been mildly unpleasant.

This scene is bound to delight audiences because of the very skillful manner in which it has made a sentimental subject seem absurd without losing sight of its inherent sentimentality. Mabel must convince us that Tommy really does want to propose to her, and she must also show us how naïve that desire is. If she accomplishes that much, she is certain of success.

ON BEING TOO FREQUENTLY PROPOSED TO

There are chairs RC and LC. Mabel Chiltern stands C, facing Lady Chiltern, who is on her right. Mabel holds an elaborate fan, which she keeps constantly in motion, and which, by its motion, punctuates and emphasizes what she has to say. Her opening sentence contains a mixture of boredom, annoyance, a sense of remote but possible scandal, and the desire to share one's troubles with a sympathetic listener. As many as possible of these attitudes should be crowded into the opening "Well."

Well, Tommy has proposed to me again.

Shrugs her shoulders, bats her eyelashes, and crosses DLC, the fan going rapidly.

Tommy really does nothing but propose to me.

Turns toward Gertrude, pointing her fan at her on the word "night."

He proposed to me last night in the music-room,

Dede Ward as Mabel: "Tommy really does nothing but propose to me."

Fanning herself again.

    when I was quite unprotected,

Left hand held to shoulder height, palm out, gesturing toward the left, suggesting the existence of a trio in some imprecise place or other.

    as there was an elaborate trio going on.

Holds the top of the fan with her left hand and smiles at Gertrude, leaning forward slightly.

    I didn't dare to make the smallest repartee, I need hardly tell you.

Pulls her head back, and on the word "stop" opens her left palm in a gesture of stopping.

    If I had, it would have stopped the music at once.

Crosses RC.

    Musical people are so absurdly unreasonable.

Turns toward Gertrude in the manner of one revealing a confidence, while at the same time sitting down.

    They always want one to be perfectly dumb at the very moment when one is longing to be absolutely deaf.

Appears to be preoccupied with arranging her dress so that it is as neatly draped about her as possible.

    Then he proposed to me in broad daylight this morning in front of that dreadful statue of Achilles.

Facing Gertrude, and left hand gesturing in her direction.

    Really, the things that go on in front of that work of art are quite appalling. The police should interfere.

Looks out toward the audience and sighs, indicating that she is contemplating another ordeal that she has gone through.

    At luncheon I saw by the

Looks toward Gertrude in such manner as to underline the word "glare."

    glare in his eye that he was going to propose again,

Looks out toward the audience and fans herself.

    and I just managed to check him in time by assuring him that I was a bimetallist.

Rises, crosses DR.

    Fortunately I don't know what bimetallism means.

Turns toward Gertrude, speaks triumphantly.

    And I don't believe anybody else does either.

Fans herself again, speaking very happily.

> But the observation crushed Tommy for ten minutes. He looked quite shocked.

Crosses DLC, speaking slowly and thoughtfully.

> And then Tommy is so annoying in the way he proposes.

Turns to Gertrude, speaking with great certainty.

> If he proposed at the top of his voice, I should not mind so much. That might produce some effect on the public.

Crosses around up behind chair, LC. Feels the upholstery of it daintily with her left hand while with her right hand she continues to fan herself at a medium rate. Her voice is again thoughtful.

> But he does it in a horrid confidential way. When Tommy wants to be romantic he talks to one just like a doctor. I am very fond of Tommy, but his methods of proposing are quite out of date.

Crosses around in front of the chair, pointing her fan at Gertrude.

> I wish, Gertrude, you would speak to him, and tell him that once a week is quite often enough to propose to anyone, and

Spreads her hands in front of her in order to attain a particularly beautiful pose.

> that it should always be done in a manner that attracts

Smiles, seats herself with the greatest possible elegance.

> some attention.

VOCAL AND PHYSICAL CHARACTERIZATION

Nearly everything that has been said about Belinda applies also to Mabel, with two exceptions. Mabel's beauty is more natural, though she is just as conscious of it; and her dress is not as full as Belinda's, though she, too, is conscious of how it looks and carefully arranges it for maximum effect whenever possible.

Mabel should have a light, highly inflected voice that is very pleasant to listen to. Its prettiness, however, should contain no suggestion of depth of character. This empty quality may be achieved by giving the voice an upward inflection at the end of most phrases, and, in general, by allowing it to touch the words lightly without giving them too much weight or warmth. There is a smile in Mabel's voice; but it is a smile of elegance, perhaps of gaiety, but never of warmth. Her voice should never take on so much lightness, however, that it seems merely silly. Like many of Wilde's characters, Mabel is extremely serious about not being serious, and her dedication to the cause of frivolity gives her voice drive and energy.

All these qualities may make it appear that Mabel has none of the simplicity we have described earlier. However, at a time when every upper class young lady was expected to move and to speak in an elegant manner, Mabel would have seemed quite simple and natural. The secret is to make everything she does seem second nature to her. This will best be achieved with enough practice so that every gesture and every inflection becomes a habit.

BIBLIOGRAPHY

In addition to the complete texts of the plays from which these scenes are taken, and the other books in this series, the following may prove useful.

Anderson, Virgil A., *Training the Speaking Voice,* Oxford University Press, New York, 1942. One of the best books available on the technique of voice production, it offers a complete technical explanation of the vocal apparatus and the best means of using it.

Blunt, Jerry, *Stage Dialects,* Chandler Publishing Company, 1967. The fundamental information necessary for learning eleven different dialects is here. Recorded tapes designed to accompany the book are also available.

Bowman, Walter Parker, and Ball, Robert Hamilton, *Theatre Language, a Dictionary of Terms in English of the Drama and Stage from Medieval to Modern Times,* Theatre Arts Books, New York, 1961. More than 3,000 words and phrases used in connection with the theatre are defined here. For less exacting purposes, there is a good glossary in Ommanney's *The Stage and the School.*

Browne, E. Martin (ed.), *Religious Drama 2,* Living Age Books, New York, 1958. The complete texts of twenty-one medieval mystery and morality plays, including *Everyman.* Reading through these would be the best possible way to absorb the spirit necessary for the effective acting of *Everyman.*

Campbell, Oscar James (ed.), and Quinn, Edward G. (assoc. ed.), *The Reader's Encyclopedia of Shakespeare,* Thomas Y. Crowell Company, New York, 1966. The most comprehensive reference book on Shakespeare available. There are interpretations of all the plays, as well as articles on Shakespeare's theatre, sources and references. Especially interesting are the articles on Shakespearean actors of all periods.

Cole, Toby, and Chinoy, Helen Krich (eds.), *Actors on Acting,* Crown Publishers, New York, 1949. More than 100 actors and writers explain in their own words their theories about acting.

Cunningham, J. S., *Pope: The Rape of the Lock,* Barron's Educational Series, Inc., Great Neck, New York, 1961. Background information and a critical evaluation.

Funke, Lewis, and Booth, John E. (eds.), *Actors Talk About Acting* (2 vols.), Avon Books, New York, 1961. Fourteen interviews with contemporary actors that give each actor an opportunity to express his views at considerable length.

Granville-Barker, Harley, and Harrison, G. B. (eds.), *A Companion to Shakespeare Studies,* Anchor Books, Garden City, 1960. Fifteen articles by scholars help to place Shakespeare's plays in a critical and historical context.

Harrison, G. B., *Elizabethan Plays and Players,* Ann Arbor Books, Ann Arbor, 1956. A scholarly discussion of the theatre of Shakespeare's time, and the playwrights and actors who made it what it was.

Hartnoll, Phyllis (ed.), *The Oxford Companion to the Theatre,* Oxford University Press, New York, 1951. One of the best reference books on all phases of theatre.

Joseph, Bertram, *Acting Shakespeare,* Theatre Arts Books, New York. An investigation of Shakespeare's background in learning to write plays leads to some helpful information on how to act Shakespeare for contemporary audiences so as to reveal the rich verbal structure of the plays.

Joseph, Bertram, *The Tragic Actor,* Theatre

Arts Books, New York. A history of English tragic acting with specific reference to the great tragic actors and helpful information for the contemporary actor.

Lewis, C. S., *A Preface to Paradise Lost,* Galaxy Books, New York. One of the finest interpretations of Milton's great epic, giving much of the religious and philosophical background of the poem.

Nelms, Henning, *Play Production,* College Outline Series, New York, 1950. A comprehensive and easily available handbook on all phases of play production, particularly useful for the actor who wishes to be aware of those phases of play production in which he has not been trained.

Ommanney, Katharine Anne, *The Stage and the School,* McGraw-Hill Book Company, New York, 1960. A textbook that covers all phases of theatre and contains a number of scenes for several actors, as well as useful appendixes, including one on considering a theatrical career.

Roberts, Vera Mowry, *On Stage, A History of the Theatre,* Harper and Row, New York, 1962. A good, readable history of the theatre, which will provide a valuable context into which to fit the scenes given here.

Ross, Lillian and Helen, *The Player, a Profile of an Art,* Simon and Schuster, New York, 1962. Interviews with contemporary actors have provided the basis for a large number of short articles telling how these actors feel about acting.

Senior, Dorothy, *The Life and Times of Colley Cibber,* Rae D. Henkle, New York, 1927. This book is difficult to obtain, but it provides a good picture of life in the theatre that produced Lord Foppington, and would certainly add to the understanding of that character.

Shank, Theodore J., *A Digest of 500 Plays,* The Crowell-Collier Press, New York, 1963. This book is very handy if you wish to obtain information about a great many plays of high quality. It will help you select plays you wish to perform or extract scenes from.

Shaw, Bernard, *Caesar and Cleopatra,* Penguin Books, Baltimore, 1951. Here is quite a different picture of Cleopatra, which you may wish to compare with Shakespeare's version.

Stanislavski, Constantin, *An Actor Prepares,* Theatre Arts Books, New York, 1936. The most famous book on "method" acting. After you read it, you should read Stanislavski's other two books, *Building a Character* and *Creating a Role* in order to get a complete picture of Stanislavski's theory. These highly disciplined techniques revolutionized the theatre and made possible much that we identify as "modern" in the drama.

Tillyard, E. M. W., *The Elizabethan World Picture,* Vintage Books, New York. The unconscious assumptions behind most of the literature written before about 1700 are here brilliantly set forth. If you wish to think as Shakespeare's or Marlowe's or Milton's characters thought, you should read it.

Watkins, Ronald, *On Producing Shakespeare,* W. W. Norton, New York, 1950. This book has influenced the physical arrangement of many modern productions of Shakespeare. It is one of the best explanations of the effect of the theatre on the plays.

Webster, Margaret, *Shakespeare Without Tears,* Premier Books, New York, 1957. A highly readable discussion of all Shakespeare's plays by one of the finest directors of our time.

DATE DUE			
MAR 24 '78			
DE 7 '81			
MAR 20			

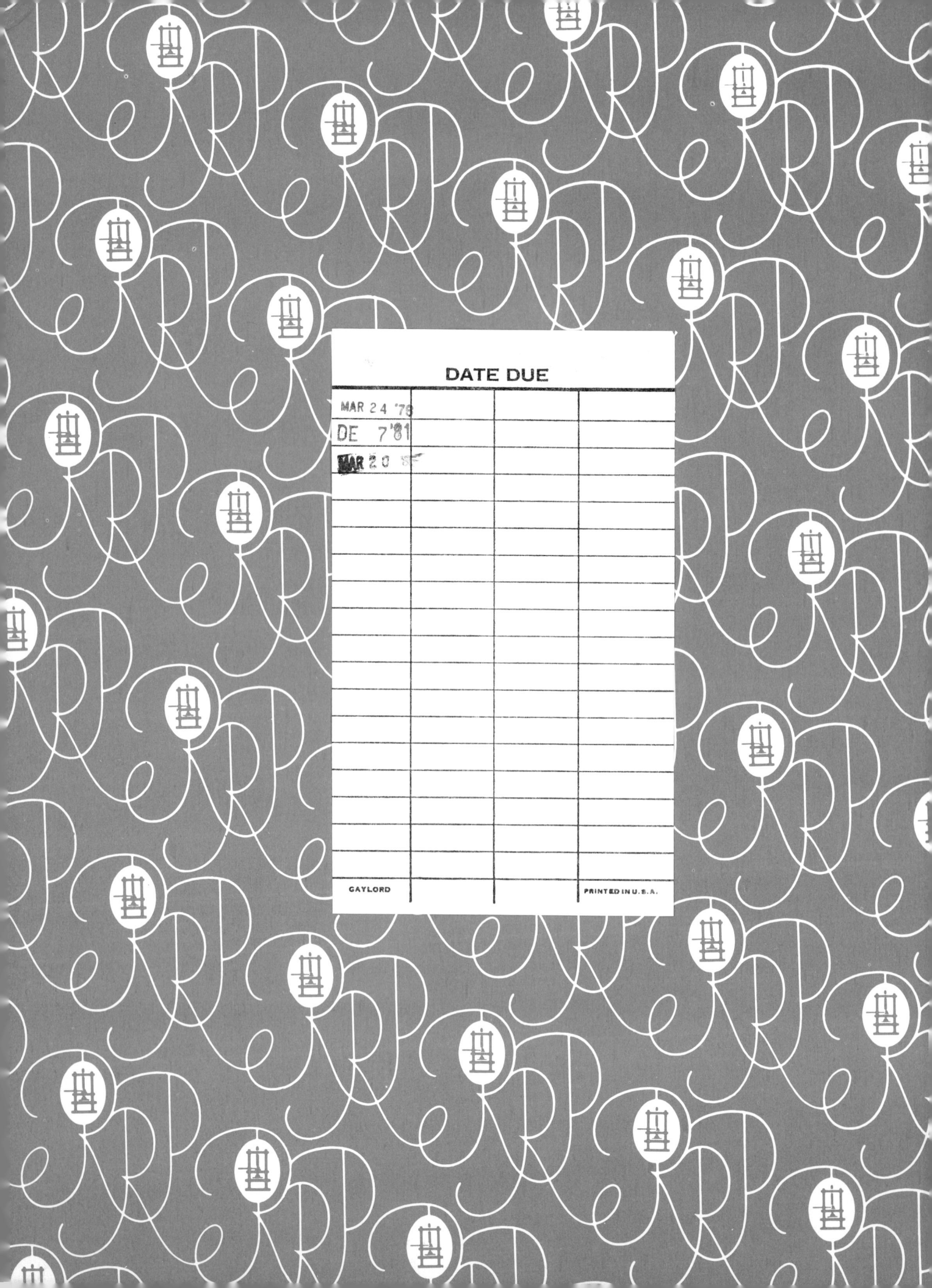